GROWING UP GREAT!

THE ULTIMATE PUBERTY BOOK FOR BOYS

GROWING UP GREAT!

SCOTT TODNEM

ILLUSTRATED BY ANJAN SARKAR

ROCKRIDGE
PRESS

Interior and Cover Designer: Stephanie Sumulong
Art Producer: Sara Feinstein
Editor: Susan Randol
Production Editor: Andrew Yackira
Illustrations © 2019 Anjan Sarkar
Author photo courtesy of © Ashley Summers

ISBN: Print 978-1-64152-464-3 | eBook 978-1-64152-465-0

This book is dedicated to my children,
my family, and all of my students who have
trusted me to be the co-captain in their
journey of growing up great.

CONTENTS

NAVIGATING LIFE CAN BE TRICKY. Friends, family, school, your health—wave after wave of responsibilities come your way as you try to stay afloat. There you are, the captain of your own ship, wondering if you can manage your way through the uncharted waters. Life priorities can drag you in different directions like the currents of an ocean—some are enjoyable, others are much more challenging. You're at the helm and steering from schoolwork to hobbies, from house chores to social

life, all with the impending physical and emotional storm of—*gasp!*—puberty.

All right, let's not get carried away. Life isn't exactly a movie trailer. There's no deep, booming voice narrating puberty for boys, like, *"In a world that is changing, one boy must journey across the ocean of adolescence on the waves of puberty into . . . MANHOOD."* That'd be weird, right? Actually, maybe that would be cool. Anyway, back to real life here.

The first thing to know about growing up is that you don't need to have it all figured out. It's okay to learn as you go. Even when you get older and gain more responsibility, never worry about having everything perfectly under control. Face it: No captain knows every little detail of their journey ahead of time. The truth is that life is a wonderful challenge, changes and all. If any of it gets overwhelming, stay confident that it will only be temporary. Think about all the great things you have going on right now. Puberty won't change that. It will change *you*, but it won't change the fact that you can remain healthy and happy through adolescence.

I know this because I am a Health Education teacher. I work with hundreds of students each year as they manage the time of life between childhood and adulthood. For boys working their way through middle school, I help them successfully handle things with accurate information, valid resources, and a whole bunch of humor. (You'll notice I'm kind of sarcastic. I might even call you dude, dude.) Plus, I think I have a knack for simply listening and understanding what kids are going through. We have a lot of fun in my classes because health and wellness are all about students themselves. I'm guessing that's why you picked up this book—it's all about you! Smart move, my friend.

You'll notice a theme throughout our topics: knowledge is power. With facts and an understanding of your body, you'll find out puberty isn't that bad. It's actually really exciting because it means you are growing up. Moving from childhood into adulthood with a strong, confident appreciation for yourself is what we will simply term "growing up great." You know the concept of respect, I'm sure. Did you know that respect starts with yourself? Self-respect means you treat yourself with pride and you know you have worth. Self-respect transfers into all other parts of life, like physical health and social relationships. *Growing up great* will mean having self-respect, but it will also mean treating others with respect. Obviously, no one is the same. Even with similarities, people are unique in their thoughts, feelings, and actions. Well, no *body* is the same, either. And we definitely don't grow up the same. Respecting yourself and others along the way is the mark of a true adult. (Yes, even if that adult says "dude" a lot.)

As we take on some tough topics together, you might realize you have more questions. Hopefully this book will allow you to open the lines of communication with your parents or guardians. Be careful about simply searching for things on the Internet. You've probably seen how it works—sites can pop up that are hard to understand, images or video might have content that you weren't quite ready to see, or worse, you might get information that is flat-out incorrect. Later on, I will offer some websites that can help so you aren't lost in the strange depths known as the World Wide Web. Instead, after reading these chapters, check in with a trusted adult, as well as your doctor, to get the additional facts you need. After all, adults are just grown-up kids. (Some of us might be big and tall but still just a kid at heart. Not naming any names, of course.)

This book is organized so that we cover the basics first, like what puberty is and the growth to expect during that time. Then we'll examine some details of the way a boy's body tends to develop. We will start small, noting the first changes that occur in height, weight, and hair growth, and then we'll work toward the bigger items like mood swings, diet and exercise, and genital changes. (Hey, what's going on down there?) All of the changes will be discussed in terms of overall health and well-being, with a focus on proper hygiene, managing emotions, and maintaining privacy. Phew! That's a lot to cover, but you deserve it. Plus, the glossary in the back of the book will help with any terms or phrases that might be new.

Through it all, I want to assure you of something: you got this. As your virtual co-captain, I will never steer you wrong. With time, and help from this book, you'll manage just fine. Consider this your guide, a navigation chart, for *growing up great*. Aye, aye, Captain? So climb aboard, because this is a journey worth taking.

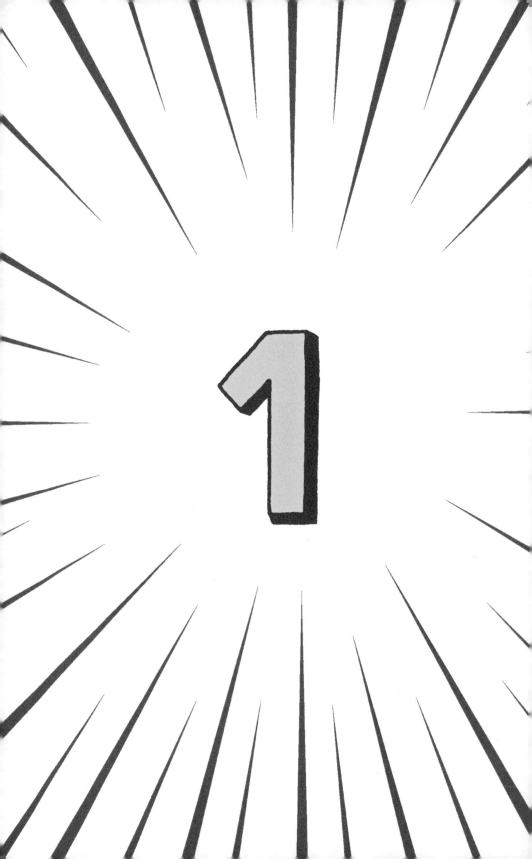

THESE CHANGING TIMES

As you've grown through childhood, you may have already noticed changes in yourself. Or perhaps you know changes are on the way and you're not quite sure what to expect. Maybe someone else in your life noticed you are changing and they picked up this book for you. Fist bump to them; they care! Whatever the case, you are here for some information. And you deserve the truth. Let's be honest; your friends don't know everything, even if they pretend to. In this chapter, we'll cover some basics on puberty without assuming what you do or don't know. Oh, and prepare yourself—there may be some words here and throughout the book that make you giggle. Totally fine. But we'll always use the correct and appropriate terms so that you have the facts. Remember: Knowledge is power. Let's dive into the basics about these changing times.

PUBERTY AND ADOLESCENCE

Everyone goes through puberty. However, people don't often talk about it. For one reason or another, people sometimes shy away from discussing their changing bodies. It could be because, in a lot of ways, puberty is a personal and private experience. Or it could be that people are afraid of saying something wrong or sounding silly, and no one likes being embarrassed. In some cases, talking about puberty might be thought of as naughty, inappropriate, or somehow dirty. Well, that couldn't be further from the truth. Puberty is not wrong, dirty, or even weird. It could feel slightly embarrassing, but talking about things in an open and honest way can help with that. (Just like we're doing in this book. Cool?) Without puberty, we wouldn't grow up and be able to reproduce. Reproduction is the process where living organisms make offspring, or more of their kind. Put simply, without reproduction, there are no humans! As you can see, puberty is a normal and necessary part of life.

What Is Puberty?

Puberty is the time in life when a person develops from a child into an adult. It is a period of physical growth when the body sexually matures and becomes able to reproduce. What that means for boys is that they will start looking and sounding more like men. The reason for this is both simple and complex. On one hand, this process means the brain is simply doing its job. It is telling the rest of the body to produce specific chemicals known as hormones in order to grow and mature. One specific hormone is testosterone, which causes most of the changes boys experience in puberty. Testosterone is produced in the testicles and is responsible for masculine characteristics such as body hair, muscle growth, and a deepened voice.

A detailed explanation is more complicated, of course, because there's more than just testosterone at play here. The hormones in the body need a specific balance to produce the right effect. The science of how the body works is incredible, and you will probably study more in school—especially as you get into higher-level classes like biology. For now, it's enough to understand that the brain and body are doing their jobs. So wipe that sweat off your forehead. There's no book report here.

What Is Adolescence?

Adolescence is the time between the beginning of puberty and adulthood. Sometimes the terms puberty and adolescence go hand in hand. The term adolescence generally refers to more than just physical growth, however—it includes social and emotional growth as well. Adolescence is a transition where the body is preparing for the rest of life. Puberty is a part of that preparation. You'll see both terms show up quite a bit as you read.

Wear Your Own Genes

Quick science lesson here. A main factor in the changes a boy experiences through puberty is his genetics. Genetics, or genes, are the characteristics inherited from biological parents. (No, not "jeans," like your pants: *genes!*) A similar term you might already know is heredity—the passing of traits from parents to children. Genes include the code that was written to form, well, you! We inherit genes from each parent, which pair together in a unique way to provide a map for the body so it can grow and continue to exist.

You will also come to hear terms like chromosomes and DNA (deoxyribonucleic acid). These describe the microscopic makeup of a person. Again, this can get pretty complicated, but it deserves mention. Genes are on chromosomes, which contain DNA. This all comes back to the fact that genes are the instructions for you. Those instructions? Before you, they were never seen in the history of the world. You are utterly and entirely unique. Wear those genes proudly, since no one has ever been you, and no one will ever be you.

From here on out, the term "parents" will also include guardians, since all families can look slightly different. Unless I am specifically drawing attention to birth parents, the word "parents" will encompass all caretakers.

What Should I Expect?

You should expect your genes to function in a similar way to those of your biological parents. Meaning, you will grow up to look and even act a little like your birth mother and father. But because of your environment—your surroundings while growing up—you will develop into a different person than your parents. You are one part *nature* and one part *nurture*. Our nature is how we are born. Genetics, remember? In contrast, when a growing child is nurtured, it means they are taken care of by a guardian. We nurture young kids by providing for their physical health (food, shelter, and safety), their mental health (emotions, intelligence, and life lessons), and their social health (family, friends, and even larger groups in society).

You are born with some foundations for growth, but that doesn't mean your future has already been set. The genetic code written to tell your body how to grow is only a general outline. Not everything is set out for you. Your choices and behavior play into how you remain healthy through adolescence. Even then, there could be some variance in how you grow. Think of yourself like a plant seed. Fertile soil and a safe environment might exist, but rain and sunshine also play a part, and those can definitely vary day to day. Likewise, your body has a good plan all set within its genes, but things like when you start puberty and what changes you see will vary between peers, siblings, and parents.

In basic terms, you can expect to see physical growth changes in height and weight. Expect to see hair growth in the armpits, on the face, and in the pubic area. Expect size change in the reproductive organs known as the penis and testicles. Expect muscle development. Expect a deeper voice. Expect acne. Expect mood swings, energy changes, and maybe even an attraction to other people. Expect to feel grown up in some ways and still a kid in others. In general, these changes will begin anywhere as early as age 9 and as late as age 14. Puberty changes will be complete as young as age 16 to as old as the early 20s. It is best if you don't expect anything specific at a certain age, however, because boys will have a different amount of growth and a different order of changes compared to peers. These changes will be thoroughly discussed in upcoming chapters.

What Is Normal?

A common question from anyone going through puberty is, "Am I normal?" It's a valid concern, and one that proves we all have a basic need to belong. We want to know that everything we experience is okay. We don't like to feel alone, especially while going through the body changes of puberty. First of all, pretty much everything during puberty is normal. Boys are always changing at their own rate. Differences are allowed. Boys will experience ups and downs during the puberty process. This includes growth spurts, more body hair, and reproductive development. This also includes pauses in growth, like little rest breaks in the changes they observe. These are the ebbs and flows in the ocean of adolescence that make every boy normal.

It is also normal to wonder if you measure up to other boys. You'll naturally wonder about height, body hair, penis size, vocal tone, and musculature. It's okay to wonder if your body is growing correctly. Comparing yourself to others is a slippery slope, though, so be careful of that. We will talk more about some specific numbers in chapter 2 (page 17) and beyond, but also keep an eye out for statistics in the sidebars throughout the book. Statistics are numbers, my friend. But you knew that.

POWER IN NUMBERS

There are around 1.5 billion adolescents in the world aged 10–18. That's a lot of people going through puberty! Boys make up around half of those numbers, which means over 300 million boys are starting the process of *growing up great*. You are definitely not alone. Boys tend to experience the start of puberty between ages 9 and 14. Most will end puberty by ages 16–18. Keep in mind that everyone grows at their own pace, however. Changes can even continue into a person's 20s.

GROWING AND CHANGING

In puberty, the body can change at an alarming rate. Even with the fluctuations in pacing, this is generally a time in which growth is fast and furious. The only time you grew at a faster rate was when you were an infant. And it should go without mention: You are much different now. (Dare we bring up diapers?) You can plan on coming through the other side of puberty a different person as well. Change is good, remember?

It is important to know what to be on the lookout for during adolescence. Aim your focus straight ahead, mate; the first waves of puberty are about to hit.

First Signs of Puberty

The beginning of puberty will most likely be several small changes that happen simultaneously. Little milestones will also continue throughout adolescence. For most boys, the first signs of puberty are minor— the shoulders look a bit more defined, the voice has deepened slightly, or height has increased in the last six months. Maybe the testicles have gotten just a bit larger as the skin of the reproductive organs darkens. Perhaps there is new hair on the sides of the pubic bone or just above the penis. While these all mark the onset of puberty, they will certainly not follow the same order for each person.

One simple way the body prepares for adulthood is to grow in height and gain more weight. Testosterone, the main hormone in action during puberty, will cause boys to gain significant body size. With an increase in height will come an increase in weight, as we will cover in the next chapter. This might first be noticeable in the hands or feet. Those extremities might grow faster than other parts of the body in the beginning, causing some boys to feel a bit clumsy. Muscle mass will start to develop; shoulders, legs, and chest will gain size and definition. You may notice some growing pains in the joints or muscles, which is a sign that things are working internally to create a bigger you.

Some other signs that puberty has begun are changes in your voice. Prepare for some cracks in your vocals at this time. Family members love to poke fun at this. It's cool; they love you. Others might notice in school or community events, too. (Your comeback? *"No cracks about my voice, please."* Then give them a punny smile.)

Body hair will begin looking and feeling coarser. Arm and leg hair might become darker and more obvious. Armpit hair will be fine at first, and then thicker in time. Pubic hair will start in small patches right above the penis and below the belly button. This hair can start to sprout upward toward the stomach and on the inner thighs, as well as on the nipples. Speaking of nipples, there might be some more sensitivity or slight swelling of the nipples or breast tissue of the chest.

Your skin might start to feel more oily or greasy. More sweating will now occur, especially in the armpits and maybe even in the crotch. (You know, that groin area down there?) With hormones causing changes in sweat and body hair, it will now be important to keep up with hygiene. Washing your face, armpits, penis, and testicles thoroughly each day and night will help keep acne and odor at a minimum. Acne, including pimples or "zits," is inevitable: it's going to happen. Body odor will be more common because of the increase in sweat and bacteria. You can help things by keeping clean, which we will cover more later on.

The genitals, or external reproductive organs, will gain a little size at the beginning of puberty. The testes, or testicles, will enlarge first. Testicles aren't so much "balls"—you'll notice that they're more oval-shaped and that they become even more sensitive as puberty begins. (Hard to believe, right? Keep them safe!) The scrotum is the sac of skin that contains the testes. This will enlarge and thicken as well, and all of the genitals might turn darker in skin tone. As the testicles and scrotum gain size, the penis will follow, and you may begin to experience erections. A relaxed, "soft" state is known as a flaccid penis. A stimulated penis is known as erect. Although a slang term is "boner," we will use the term erection, since, technically, there is no bone there. An erection is when the penis becomes hard and stands up and out from the body because it is filled with blood. This is normal and can occur for no reason at all besides the fact that hormones are helping the body grow.

We will discuss all of these changes, and more, in upcoming chapters.

Puberty Timeline

After that first wave of puberty, you may be wondering what else is to come. Boys often feel prepared for more, especially if they feel stronger or they like how tall or mature they are starting to look. It's like dessert—if some is good, more is better! Hold on there, buddy. Remember the body is working with its own instructions, so the genes inside you have the ultimate say. You can't rush things, and you can't really slow them down, either. You just have to roll with the punches.

Here is a general outline, while keeping in mind that everyone has a specific timeline within themselves. These estimates might vary.

AGES 9-12: Hormone levels increase. Body size changes; muscles develop. Height and weight increase. Voice starts to change. Body hair thickens.

AGES 10-14: Body size continues to increase. Underarm and pubic hair become more prominent. Sweat and body odor increase. Regular hygiene becomes necessary. The testicles and scrotum grow first; the penis follows. Erections become more regular. Nipples may become fuller and more sensitive.

AGES 11-16: Height and body size increase. Pubic hair is getting darker and spreading. Underarm hair becomes more full. Hygiene needs continue through puberty and into adulthood. Chest and facial hair begin, especially on the upper lip and sideburns. Muscle mass increases. Voice really starts to change and deepen. The testicles and penis continue to grow. Erections and wet dreams may occur.

AGES 12-17: The genitals continue to grow and deepen in skin pigment color. Wet dreams may occur more regularly. Facial features and muscle mass look more mature. Body and facial hair are noticeable and may be in need of grooming. Height increase is slowing down. Skin continues to become oily, and face and body acne may be present.

AGES 16-18+: Boys reach their full adult height. Pubic hair, facial hair, and genitals look like an adult. Voice change is complete. Nipples are no longer as enlarged or sensitive. Hygiene and grooming needs are that of a man.

The Rate of Change

As you have read multiple times in this chapter, life changes are different for everyone. There is no way to perfectly predict a puberty timeline for each boy, but that's all right—we don't need one. A general idea of what is to come is just fine. (Besides, when have you followed all the rules?) It helps to know that everything is normal, including a varying rate of experiencing change. What is true for your friend, your neighbor, your cousin, or your brother might not be true for you. Realizing your body is doing exactly what it needs to do should hopefully help your self-respect.

YOUR CHANGING BODY

Change is good. Let's always keep that in mind. You wouldn't want to be the same today as you were at five years old. And you don't want to stay your current age forever, either. Luckily, your body is doing its job, so there's really no choice—you are aging and growing accordingly. There are some choices you do have, however, which you'll be glad to hear. Life will be a balance of both. Some things you can control. Other things your body will take care of on its own. If it feels like you can't keep up with the changes and your body is either growing too fast, or not fast enough, then it's important to remember: Normal looks different for everyone. Differences are natural. Boys might be tall and thin or short and heavy, all of which are just fine. Here's what to expect as your body size starts to change.

HEIGHT AND WEIGHT

Everyone is born with a particular body type. Humans, like all animal species, are unique from one another. Even with the same parents, siblings can look and act differently. (Have annoying brothers or sisters? Bad news, buddy: You also annoy them.) Facial features, personality, and physical characteristics like height and weight can all vary. Small babies might grow up to be taller adults. Big toddlers might thin out by their teenage years. It all depends on genetics—remember that word from chapter 1? Your genetic code will plant the seeds for how you'll grow, but what you do to take care of yourself also plays into things. Your habits with food and exercise matter. So do your habits with screen time—technology like TV, the Internet, and video games. Managing all of these choices will help boys continue to be healthy and fit through puberty.

Growth Spurts

Have you ever kept track of your height and weight? Do your parents keep a growth chart, marks on the wall, or anything similar? Besides routine visits to the doctor to record height and weight changes, it is common for families to chart the growth of children. Relatives love to point out how much you have grown since they last saw you. First of all, it's true! You are growing, even if you can't see it day to day. You're just going to have to go along with a family member who says, "Well, look at you! My, my, how you've grown." They might even joke that your pants are too short or you must have grown a foot overnight. (Insert sarcastic response here: *Really? An extra foot?! But I only have two shoes!")* Try not to be so hard on them, though. They are noticing the changes in you, and that's okay—it's exciting for them, too.

Remember, adolescence is the time between the beginning of puberty and adulthood. It's a transition where the body is preparing for the rest of life. That process might speed up or slow down at times. We will repeat this often: Everyone grows at their own pace. In general, boys can expect to start puberty changes between ages 9 and 14. During these ages, boys can hit a growth spurt where they are taller in just a matter of months. There can also be a delay in growth, where boys don't see much of a difference for a while. Expect a bit of both. This varies because of hormones, which we covered in the first chapter. A visit to the doctor's office may prove that a boy didn't grow very much since the last checkup. In other cases, a young boy might be head and shoulders above most classmates, growing out of clothes faster than he can keep track. Boys might gain as much as 6 inches or as little as 1 inch between yearly visits to the doctor. Don't worry. Your doctor will talk through a course of action if there is any concern. Otherwise, your body is working on its own timeline. You can be healthy at any height.

After a visit with your family doctor, they might find some things going on with your muscles, your joints, or your spine. If you have a high rate of growth, there can sometimes be soreness in the body we tend to call growing pains. These are usually not a concern, just a mild inconvenience to you. It's natural for that soreness to come and go a bit as the muscles keep up with the bone growth your body is experiencing. Growing pains are generally concentrated in the muscles, not the joints, so check with the doctor if your joints are bothering you. Soreness can occur in the thighs and front of the legs, in the calves and lower legs, and in the back of the knees. No big worries; they're mostly just a pain in the butt. (Get it?)

Your doctor might do a spine check to determine that the vertebrae—those small bones up and down your back—are aligned correctly. If there's an "S" or a

"C" shaped curvature present, you might be diagnosed with scoliosis, which is a common medical condition where a person's spine has a sideways curve. If this is the case, there are plenty of treatments to help with correcting that growth.

WACKY FACTS

The tallest man in recorded history was Robert Wadlow (1918–1940), who was 8 feet, 11.1 inches tall and weighed in at 490 pounds. The shortest man in history was Chandra Bahadur Dangi (1939–2015), who was 1 foot, 9.5 inches tall and weighed 32 pounds. This proves how many differences in body types there can be as boys grow into men.

Shape and Weight Changes

Just like your height will depend on your genes, so too will much of your body weight. Becoming heavier is a good thing. Your height is changing, so some of that weight gain will be bone and tissue mass—your organs are getting larger and your limbs are increasing in length. Quite a bit of your weight gain will be muscle. You will notice broader shoulders and more musculature in the chest and arms. A boy's body can have a skinnier looking muscle tone, more bulk and definition, or fat covering the growing muscles. Whatever the case, there are lots of "normal" bodies.

Some of the weight gain during puberty is body fat. Fat gets a bad rap because of the unhealthy consequences of having too much. However, the right amount of body fat (also known as adipose tissue) helps with energy storage, body temperature, vitamin absorption, and healthy skin. Some fat, called subcutaneous fat, is just under the skin and is used for warmth and cushioning. Other fat, called visceral fat, is around the internal organs to protect them. During puberty, some boys will lose the "baby fat" they carried through childhood, while others might see an increase in fat tissue. Something to know is that muscle tissue and fat tissue are different. One cannot turn into the other. Your body has a specific amount of both. The weight on the scale does not determine the makeup of your body in terms of muscle and fat mass, so realize it is only a guide. Doctors use a Body Mass Index (BMI) measurement to compare height and weight with your age. Your doctor might believe your BMI is healthy even if it's above or below average, and they will tell you and your parents if there are any weight concerns.

Healthy choices can impact your height and weight. Your fitness throughout childhood has an impact on adolescence, which in turn has an impact on adulthood. Healthy kids tend to be healthy teens. The way you eat, exercise, and sleep helps your body do what it needs. Healthy eating lets your brain manage its hormones and memory. Physical activity allows the muscles to work and grow. Sleep gives your mind and body a time to recover from all the changes that are occurring. Compared to when you were a baby, puberty is the time of life with the next-greatest growth. With that growth comes an increase in energy needs. This means you could be hungry more often and need to eat additional food throughout the week. Your body uses calories, the energy found in food, to fuel your height and weight gains. Yes, we all know those chips and soda taste great, but do your best to stick to the good stuff instead of just snack foods. And your brain might enjoy

the challenge of your favorite video game, but not at the expense of exercise or sleep. Take care of these essential needs and balance your screen time. Your growth depends on it!

Nutrition, exercise, and sleep will be covered more in chapter 5 (page 75). If you have any specific questions about height and weight, always ask your doctor.

DARE NOT TO COMPARE

It is natural to notice others. People might notice tall boys, strong boys, or the best athletes. It's common to see muscular guys portrayed as masculine and grown-up on the Internet, on TV shows, or in advertisements. With photo filters and computerized changes, keep in mind that what you see may or may not be real. And those elite athletes in professional sports? They're the best in the world. Remember that everyone changes at their own rate and has their own strengths, both physical and mental. You can always talk to a parent and your doctor about your height, weight, and rate of growth. But keep in mind that comparison is often unfair, so dare not to compare!

KEEPING IT CLEAN

Maintaining cleanliness with your body isn't as simple as it may seem. On the surface, saying something like, "Keep yourself clean!" sounds like a no-brainer, but it is definitely more complicated than that. We need to get into how to care for your body as it changes, but it all starts with some basics. After all, your plan is to roll with the changes as you *grow up great*. That's *all* the changes, my friend. Don't overlook the importance of hair care, skin care, and caring for a bunch of other basic body parts as you develop through adolescence.

Hair Care

You have known the importance of maintaining your hair since you were a kid. Your parents probably helped with this when you were young, but now it's on you. Maybe you never liked how someone else styled your hair. Or maybe you didn't care one way or the other. Well, you'll get more say in the matter now. What you do with your hair habits during adolescence will set yourself up for success in the long run. You want great hair, right? Well, head and scalp health will contribute to that.

First of all, not only does everyone have a unique hairstyle, but they also have unique hair follicles. A hair follicle is a part of the skin where the body packs old cells together. Those cells form hairs, which push through small openings, or pores, on the surface of the

skin. The shape of each hair follicle causes the style of hair; this is what contributes to determining whether your hair is straight, wavy, curly, coiled, or kinked. Much of this is genetic—hair has strong roots in our family tree. (Hair: Roots. Roots: Tree. Wow, we're on a roll here.) Hair style is closely connected with our heritage, which is a term that refers to our family background. Therefore, differences in hair types will coincide with differences in race. For instance, the hair follicles found in darker-skinned individuals are often more elongated in shape compared to the follicles found in lighter-skinned individuals. That can vary, of course. The ultimate factor is the shape of the follicle within each pore. If the follicle is round, hair will tend to grow straight. An oval follicle will create wavy hair. A hooked or elliptical-shaped follicle will give you curly or coiled hair. Interesting, right?

Your type of hair can also affect how oily your hair is. Curly-haired people may find they don't have to wash their hair as often as their straight-haired counterparts. However, curly-haired people can often experience scalp irritation and more flakes of dry skin called dandruff. There are no rigid rules on this, though, except that your hair will differ, even from your siblings.

Hair can be fine or coarse, short or long, and golden blonde to bright red to jet black—all of which can be cool. How you do yours creates a unique look to go along with your great personality, which makes grooming and hair care kind of fun. (Just don't "pore" over yourself too much—you'll want to be timely with getting prepared each day.) Whatever you decide, keep your hair clean. That might mean you shampoo only a few times a week, or it might mean you wash your hair close to every day. You might use conditioner; you might not. A parent can recommend washing habits and brand names based on their knowledge of you and your hair. Once in the shower and washing, make sure to get the shampoo to the scalp and massage just a bit with the fingertips. This helps the pores stay clean and regenerates the skin on your scalp.

After showering, some boys might go dry and natural, while some might prefer to use hair products. Again, this could be because of the type of hair you have, but it also might be because you want it styled a certain way. Oil, gel, cream, and paste are all types of hair care products you might come across. The results of each are slightly different and some could better match your hair type, so it's okay to experiment and find the best for your specific hair.

Puberty is also a time when underarm hair and pubic hair will develop. This means maintenance with your armpits and pubic area is important, too. Boys might see underarm hair sprout that is wispy and fine, or might see dark patches of small curls in the armpit. Boys might have thick, coarse hair begin on the sides of the pubic bone right below the belt line, or have thin hair at the base of the penis near the body. This all depends on body hair type determined by genes. Body hair will usually be the color of other hair that you already have, like eyebrows or leg hair. Sometimes pubic and underarm hair is a tad darker, however. No matter the color, type, or amount, keep body hair clean by scrubbing in the shower at the same time that you wash the hair on your head. Soap or shampoo will both work. This will keep those little microorganisms called bacteria at a lower number. Bacteria is what impacts body odor. Fun fact: Sweat doesn't have a smell. When sweat, or perspiration, meets bacteria on the skin, that's when a stench might start. Everyone sweats. Washing each day is a clean habit to start and to hold on to.

We will discuss pubic hair and related genital changes in depth in chapter 4 (page 57).

The Skin You're In

Did you know that your skin is considered an organ? Not only that, but it's the biggest organ of the human body. It needs to cover a lot of surface area, which means your skin makes up around 15 percent of your total body weight. Skin varies depending on the part of the body. It is the thinnest on our eyelids and the thickest on the soles of our feet and the palms of our hands. Our skin helps maintain body temperature, protects us from injury and illness, and has nerve endings that allow us to feel. That's one impressive organ.

The outer layer of skin is called the epidermis. This layer consists of cells to make us waterproof, which is, shall we say, *awesome*. The epidermis does this so we don't swell with water or other liquid we come into contact with each day. The skin still allows some absorption, which is why medical creams and ointments work, but waterproofing ourselves is an amazing feat that protects our delicate insides. The epidermis layer of cells is continuously shed and completely replaced at a rate of around once or twice a month. It has a protein that creates our fingernails and toenails, which are compacted cells that harden into the flattened shape you know.

The epidermis also contains melanin, which is a pigment that gives us the color of our skin. Melanin is the stuff that causes the skin to tan with sunlight. Sunlight also causes the body to produce vitamin D, which is why some sun exposure is healthy. Tanning too much, however, both outdoors and by artificial means such as tanning beds, causes ultraviolet (UV) radiation that raises the risk of skin irritations like sunburn, premature aging, and skin cancer. The bottom line? You're better off in your natural skin.

Each person has unique levels of melanin, which is why even siblings can have slightly different skin tones. You already know that people come in a wide variety of skin colors, from lighter, pale skin to dark brown. This has to do with genetics, and where our ancestors hail from here on Earth. As mentioned, sunlight prompts the body to produce vitamin D, but excess UV rays can harm the body, so different skin tones were a balancing act of evolution. Early humans developed lighter skin in colder places like northern Europe where sunlight wasn't as plentiful. People developed permanently darker skin in warm places—specifically around the equator, such as Africa, Central America, and the Middle East—in order to manage sun damage. These skin tone differences have lasted through countless generations and make the human species a diverse group. Be proud of the skin you're in. It represents your great heritage.

Know Sweat

The second layer of our skin is called the dermis. We talked earlier about body hair—follicles are part of the special structures in the dermis. This layer also includes nerve endings that let us feel hot and cold as well as pain, and oil to lubricate our skin to keep it from getting too dry. Other functions of the dermis include the ability to create goose bumps to raise body hair in order to trap heat in the body if it is too cold. If the body becomes too hot, sweat glands in the dermis spring into action to produce fluid on the skin's surface. This sweat is then evaporated, pulling body heat away from the body to cool down.

While the hands and feet are the sweatiest parts of the human body, you'll notice other places get sweaty, too. One well-known spot is the armpits. With puberty bringing more armpit hair to trap bacteria, you will benefit from using a deodorant or antiperspirant in the armpits to keep body odor down. Apply this in a thin layer each morning and after every shower. You might not be able to smell yourself, but it's a smart move. Hygiene helps social health, too, my friend! Find a deodorant you like that doesn't irritate your skin. Your parents might have a recommendation.

Acne and Other Skin Conditions

Washing the body is one part of personal hygiene that helps multiple issues. Particularly focus on areas you notice get sweaty throughout each day. Sweat can contribute to acne, which is the result of inflamed pores that lead to bumps on the skin. Other terms you've probably heard include pimples or zits. Some get called whiteheads and blackheads. These types of acne have a colored head to them. Acne is most common during adolescence, but it can affect any age group. Pimples during puberty pop up on the face, forehead, chest, upper back, shoulders, and even the buttocks. No area is uncommon. Acne is mainly caused by hormone changes during puberty. Most boys will get acne at one point or another, so never think it's because you are dirty or greasy. Keeping things clean can help, however. Monitor your hygiene, use simple over-the-counter creams as needed, and consult a doctor or skin expert with questions about other acne treatments.

Other skin conditions might start to show up during puberty. Some terms you may have heard from family members or classmates are eczema, psoriasis, or dermatitis. These all cause irritation on the surface of the skin. There are some other issues we should cover. You've learned a little about bacteria, those tiny colonies of living organisms. Well, there are other microorganisms to be on the lookout for during puberty. They might be microscopic, but they can cause conditions you'll be able to notice. One such microorganism is called a fungus. It can cause a foot condition commonly known as athlete's foot. This is contagious and anyone can get it, but it is often found in athletes who might share a common locker room floor. The fungal infection causes itchy, scaling skin. It usually begins between the toes but can also affect the toenails and bottoms of the feet. It is very curable. Medicine can be found at your local pharmacy or drugstore. To help prevent athlete's foot, keep your feet clean and remove sweaty socks and shoes as soon as possible after exercise.

One final type of microorganisms to mention are viruses. A virus is a microscopic particle that infects cells of the body it is living in. Viruses cause irritations like cold sores (herpes simplex virus), which are blisters around the mouth. Viruses also cause warts (human papillomavirus), which are bumps that grow on the hands, feet, and other body parts. Both cold sores and warts are somewhat uncomfortable and will often need treatment. Let your parent know what's

going on if these show up, and ask them to take you to the pharmacy or to a doctor for help. Viruses are contagious, so don't pick at anything because it can be spread. One final important note: If anything unusual shows up on the genitals, be sure to check in with your doctor for the best course of action.

So, there's the skinny on the skin. Like any other organ, take care of it, and it will take care of you.

POWER IN NUMBERS

Around 85 percent of people between the ages of 12 and 24 experience acne. Most of the time, we are tougher on ourselves than others are about any blemishes that show up. Stay positive that if pimples pop up, others may not notice at all. Everyone has their own things going on! The same is true with other skin conditions. One in 10 boys will develop dermatitis or similar issues at some point in adolescence.

Eyes and Ears

The human senses are incredible, you know? Sometimes we overlook that fact. Our senses work together to give us input on our daily reality. If you have the gift of all of them—sight, smell, taste, hearing, touch, and a bunch of other complex senses like a sense of balance and a sense of pain—then you know the importance of each. This is especially true when you need to call upon something specific. If you have lost any senses, or have been born with different abilities than others, you certainly appreciate what you do have. Often, your other senses work a little better as a result. Taking care of your senses is like everything else we have discussed in this chapter—the small efforts you put in to your daily hygiene and grooming habits all pay off big in the long run. You are one amazing human being. Take nothing for granted and you'll continue to grow up great.

What's up first? Let's see . . . your eyes! Your vision will undoubtedly be tested either at your yearly doctor's visits, at school, or both. If you wear glasses or contact lenses, you already realize you'll get an update on your eyesight each year. As you age through adolescence, those checkups will continue to ensure your prescription matches the strength of your sight. Keep your glasses or contacts clean and safe so you don't create extra, unnecessary costs. Prescription sports glasses might be an option if you are active. They will make sure your eyes are protected and the glasses won't fall off during practices and games. Whether you wear glasses or not, you'll benefit from giving your eyes a break from phones, tablets, video games, and other screens. Be especially careful of being in pitch-dark rooms where you have a bright screen in your face for hours and hours straight. (Chances are you knew that already— just trying to keep an eye out for you here! *Wink*)

No matter where you are right now, stop and listen. Do you hear that? If so, thank your ears! Even recognizing silence is a gift from your sense of hearing. If you've been prone to ear infections from a young age, keep up with cleanliness through adolescence. Infections are super painful. During showers, as you're washing your hair, give the ears a quick rinse as well. Scrub the outsides and then cause a little movement by pushing and pulling lightly on the earlobes to help release any loose earwax. Be very careful with cotton swabs, since you can poke and damage the eardrum. Keep earbud and headphone volume and total use at a minimum, and definitely take them off during sleep. Wearing earbuds or headphones for just an hour will increase the bacteria in your ear by 700 times! Gross, right? You will generally do hearing tests at the same time as vision tests, so your school nurse or family doctor will be able to guide you if you have any hearing issues that need to be addressed.

Mouth and More

Your mouth is a busy place during puberty. You will lose the remaining primary teeth you have—what you usually refer to as your baby teeth. Your permanent teeth only come in one set, so take good care of these and your smile will shine as brightly as your future. During these years, an increase of bacteria will exist on your teeth, gums, and tongue. This is normal. While some

of the bacteria can be harmful, most are actually not, and some are even helpful. Certain types of bacteria, however, multiply and grow if they're not removed. They combine with food particles and create a film called plaque. Plaque can harden into tartar, which causes gum disease. Not good. Plaque can also combine with sugar to produce the acid that causes cavities. To prevent gum disease and cavities, you need to remove plaque. The way to do this is to brush and floss every day. Dentists say that the minimum time you should spend brushing your teeth is 2 minutes, two to three times a day. Brushing won't remove all the plaque between your teeth, under the gums, or under braces. (And speaking of braces, be sure to follow your orthodontist's specific directions for cleaning your teeth and taking care of your braces.) Remember, you'll also need to floss these spaces at least once a day. If you struggle with these habits, start small with helpful reminders like putting the floss out next to your toothbrush. Don't like dental care? Grin and bear it, dude. After a while, it just becomes another quick hygiene habit.

While we're at it, let's make sure to mention one last way to keep your changing body healthy and clean. Wash your hands! Your sense of touch, particularly in the hands, is such a common and important part of the human experience. You're not a little kid anymore, so keep those hands out of your mouth and your fingers out of your nose. Wash for a good 30 seconds multiple times a day to keep germs away. If you don't know already, learn how to use nail clippers to keep your fingernails trimmed and clean from dirt. And no biting! This is more than just for looks. It all helps control a lot of what we discussed in recent sections—acne, eye, and ear infections, and dental health.

LOOKING AND SOUNDING OLDER

Throughout puberty, many of the changes in the body include what are called secondary sex characteristics. Primary sex characteristics include changes to the genitals—the penis and testes—and will be discussed in depth in chapter 4 (page 57). Secondary sex characteristics, on the other hand, include pretty much everything else that changes with puberty.

Besides height and weight, two outward changes that occur in boys throughout puberty are a deepening voice and the growth of body hair. Obviously, your face and voice can be seen and heard. Therefore, any changes are noticeable to others, so you can expect to hear about them. Family and friends don't mean any harm—they are noticing that you're growing up, and that's okay. We started off the last chapter with this in mind and will repeat it often: Change is good. And knowledge is power.

As you grow to look and sound older, you might be wondering how to manage things like facial hair and speaking in public. In this section, we will highlight what you need to know about your body as you balance outward changes and self-confidence in your journey through puberty.

TO SHAVE, OR NOT TO SHAVE?

These outward changes will come in a variety of orders, but first up for our focus: facial hair. That peach fuzz from childhood is going to start thickening up more at the sideburns, the upper lip, and maybe even the chin. From there it will spread. Some boys grow facial hair that fills in evenly; many do not. This is one characteristic that will take years to complete. A lot of new hair will be sparse around the face. You may have parts of the mustache show up first, you may have longer sideburns, or you may have chin and neck

hair. Depending on culture and religion, shaving body hair may not be condoned. There are ways to care for facial hair, if that's something you are allowed and motivated to do.

Contrary to popular belief, shaving won't cause body hair to grow back faster or thicker. You won't create more hair by using a razor, but shaving will be unnecessary until puberty really causes facial hair to grow. Just be careful! Razor blades are razor sharp.

Decisions, Decisions

There are several styles of razors and plenty of name brands to choose from. Like with any product, companies will advertise that they are the best and brag that their product is the one you need. There are razors with one blade or two blades, all the way up to four and five blades. There are shaving creams, shaving gels, and aftershave lotions. There are even small combs and brushes for facial hair. In the end it's about what works for you. Generic brands are also worth trying because they can offer the same or similar product for less. You can ask a father or guardian, an older brother, or even your friends for advice on what works for them. But you'll notice that you will have to try a few different things out to see what works for you.

Generally, a double-blade razor is a good starting point and does the job just fine. Don't purchase anything expensive until you know for certain what works for your face. Shaving cream is a moisturizer, so you might choose to use one, or you might find it just as good to shave with hot water. Some men shave over a sink with cream and hot water, others shave in the shower to allow the steam to help open the pores and wet down their whiskers. Either way, a mirror helps so you don't miss a spot. You can even find small mirrors that suction to the wall of the shower, if that's your choice.

How Do I Shave?

Notice the direction that your facial hairs are pointing. If unsure, you can run your fingers across each part of your face to feel for the path that offers least resistance against your fingers or fingernails. Shave with that direction first. This is known as shaving with the grain.

For the most part, that is downward on the face, from the sideburns to the neck, from the nose to the lips, from the lips to the chin, and down the neck toward the collar of your shirt. Often, the hair turns a bit to point sideways at the chin and neck, so that might mean shaving with the grain along the jawbone toward the ear, and from your Adam's apple to the side of your throat.

If using a gel or cream, still make sure to wet the face first. A dry shave will pull at the hairs and hurt quite a bit. It will also irritate the skin more. Apply just a thin layer of shaving cream on the areas you need to shave. (Fight the urge to make a huge, white, shaving cream beard. Okay, maybe try it just once.) If shaving with just soap and water, you might want to take a few minutes to get the face wet before diving in with the razor. Some men choose to have a warm washcloth and hold that against the face in the moments before shaving.

Put enough pressure on the razor to cut the hair without scraping the face. Being too gentle will actually pull at the hairs instead of cutting them cleanly, and that's painful. It may take a few swipes at certain parts of the face, especially as the amount of hair increases or if it has been a while since your last shave. Get the tiny hairs out of the razor before each new pass by rinsing it under water or tapping it against the side of the sink. This helps the blades have a clear path to the surface of your face.

Once you have shaved with the grain of your facial hair, you can then choose to go back over the same areas against the grain. A lot of times this means upward, holding the razor upside down with the handle up. This shave can cut the hair off closer to the skin, but it creates a higher chance of something called razor burn. This is a painful irritation where the hair drops below the first layer of skin and creates bumps or ingrown hair. Besides being sore, these bumps look a bit like pimples and can even develop into permanent scar tissue over time. If razor burn occurs, back off from shaving for a few days and try a new route—stop after shaving with the grain and see how your face reacts. Razor burn is especially common on the neck where there are more wrinkles and folds. This is where the skin tends to be more sensitive. Creams can help, but it's about the shaving process. Always ask a trusted adult if you need more advice.

Electric razors are also an option when shaving. Some boys find success with these, while others find that the blades of the electric trimmer create more razor burn. Again, your personal experience will tell you what's best, and you may choose to test the various types out if financially possible. When in doubt, a simple razor and warm water is the perfect starting point. Along with your grown-up shaving habit, be sure to be courteous afterward and rinse the whiskers off the side of the sink and down the drain. Keep the sink or shower clean for the next family member—they might compliment you on both your cleanliness and your smooth shave. Win-win, dude.

POWER IN NUMBERS

Face the facts: When and how boys start to shave is all over the map. On average, boys will notice new facial hair before age 16. For some, it's a major milestone. For others, it's not that big a deal. It's okay if you feel excited, annoyed, or indifferent. Here are some shaving memories from a few men who have faced what you will.

"I remember all my friends were shaving but I hadn't grown any facial hair. One of my friends suggested I should shave and that would help me grow a beard. It didn't work. In my twenties, I started growing more facial hair and it turns out I actually dislike it. Just proves there is no reason to rush anything."
– Karl C.

"I ended up growing facial hair before my classmates. Some friends were impressed, while others told me to shave it. Because of my background and my parents, I didn't shave until age 16. I got used to it, and my classmates did as well. It just became part of who I was while growing up."
– Sachin S.

"I'm not particularly hairy, and I might have been one of the last of my friends to need to shave. Even now, growing sideburns or a beard takes me forever! When I was younger that might have been a concern to me, but now I realize that we all have different levels of hairiness."
– Andy M.

CHEST HAIR AND OTHER CHEST CHANGES

You've heard of chess, right? Well, puberty brings about a *chest* match in the body, with a lot of moving parts. Besides facial hair, other outward changes that might be noticeable to others revolve around a boy's chest. The musculature in the torso—namely the upper chest muscles known as pectorals—will gain strength and size. You can plan on broader shoulders to go along with a bigger chest. This will take time, so don't expect to wake up one day and magically be able to do 100 push-ups in a row. Strength and size of the chest muscles will differ because of genetics, but if you can stay active, eat right, and sleep enough, you will help your body develop. We will cover exercise and similar topics at length in chapter 5 (page 75).

It'll Put Hair On Your Chest

As mentioned earlier in the book, body hair will begin looking and feeling more coarse. Your torso will most likely gain some new hair, often starting in the middle of your chest, your nipples, and somewhere around your belly button. Just like facial hair, boys will usually notice some chest hair by age 16, but it won't grow in fully until the end of adolescence or even into a man's 20s. There is a running saying out there: "It'll put hair on your chest." It's just a joke that doing something difficult will make you a man. A single chest hair doesn't sprout each time you are brave or try something new. Being physically and mentally tough are fine characteristics, but they don't define masculinity. Being a gentleman or an adult also means being in tune with your emotions. We'll cover more about feelings in chapter 6 (page 95).

By adulthood, some men choose to groom their chest hair, while some leave it be. This comes down to personal preference, and you can be healthy and clean either way. Washing any chest hair is easy enough and can be done in the shower, like previously mentioned with underarm hair. Be careful of trimming chest hair, because, just like shaving facial hair, irritations can occur on the torso. Remember that body hair does not come back thicker and longer after trimming or shaving. Unlike the hair on our heads, body hair has a shorter end length, which is something called a hair's terminal length. So, no; shaving body hair won't change thickness, length, color, or growth rate. That doesn't mean you need to do so, of course. Your body. Your call.

WACKY FACTS

Prior to puberty, boys have fine hair called *vellus* hair on the face, chest, and abdomen. As puberty begins, these hairs change to terminal hair and become longer and stronger. We lose and replace around 100 body hairs a day, most of which are head hair from our scalp.

Um, Why Do I Have Nipples?

By now, you have certainly come to realize that you aren't the only one going through puberty. Not only are there millions of boys navigating their journey through adolescence, but girls are changing as well. In fact, girls often start puberty at an earlier age compared to boys. Everyone is different, as we know, so that's why we might see tall girls and short boys, or heavy boys and thin girls, or a whole bunch of other differences that can flip-flop and change in a few years' time. Many of these changes are unique to the male and female sex. Some things, however, are similar with everyone, and that's mostly because we're all human beings. As humans develop in the womb, each baby (termed a *fetus* in the months before birth), is given a similar blueprint for growth, so everyone's genetic code includes the plans for a similar body structure. Case in point: nipples! Men won't develop the genes to be able to carry children or create breast milk, making the development and function of the chest and nipples of

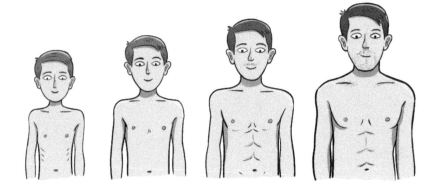

a boy during puberty quite different than that of a girl. That said, just like girls will be going through changes in their breasts and nipples, boys will see some changes in the nipples and chest tissue as well.

For pubescent boys, the chest tissue behind the nipples can harden a bit and become enlarged for months or years at a time. It may even cause the nipples to become more sensitive during this period of puberty. The term for this is *gynecomastia*, and it is fairly common in one or both nipples during puberty. Gynecomastia is caused by hormone changes. (Remember testosterone? Well, its chemical sister, estrogen, is at play here.) In most cases, the swollen breast tissue will go away without treatment, but that may take some time—it can hang around somewhere between six months and two years. During this time, the chest or nipples may look bigger because of the excess body fat. If this is a concern, check with your family doctor.

Self-Exams

While on the topic of checking for differences, we should bring up the term *self-exam*. A self-exam is exactly what it sounds like: an examination of your own body, especially as a checkup for change. You are smart for picking up this book because it is important to know which puberty changes are normal and natural. It is also crucial to know how to check for health and disease. This could be something simple like monitoring your heart rate, inspecting your teeth and gums, or checking your skin to watch for enlarged moles or unhealthy rashes. Self-exams can be done quickly each day before or after a shower or during your hygiene habits. Here are a couple of simple self-reflective questions: Does anything hurt for no reason? Am I feeling discomfort or anything out of the ordinary?

Self-exams will be brought up again in chapter 4 (page 57) as we examine puberty changes below the belt and how to keep up with testicular health.

VOCAL CHANGES

Another outward change that causes boys to seem older to others is their changing voice. If you sound older, you are often viewed as older. This can be frustrating and annoying, but it can also be empowering and exciting. With a deeper voice, you will be regarded more and more as the young man you are. However, that doesn't mean you are *feeling* mature, necessarily. It also doesn't mean you need to completely change yourself to *appear* mature. You can still enjoy your hobbies from childhood—no need to abandon your favorite toys or other interests because it feels more "grown-up." Interests will come and go. Just be you through it all. No one has ever been you, and no one will ever be you.

Vocal changes can cause confusion during puberty because there's a bit of back and forth between a higher-pitched voice and a deeper one. Let's clarify some things so you know what to expect.

What's an Adam's Apple?

The voice box has an outer wall of cartilage that is located in the middle of the throat, and this forms what is termed the "Adam's apple." A boy's Adam's apple will grow during puberty because the larynx is getting larger, providing a deeper tone to the voice. When we form words with our tongue, lips, and teeth, this sound is actually the vocal cords tightening up and moving closer together. Air from the lungs is forced between them and makes them vibrate, producing the sound of our voice.

Cracking Up

As the voice box and surrounding tissue grows, a boy's voice goes in and out of deeper pitches, causing it to have a cracking sound. This is typically experienced by age 13. The voice box will continue to grow and, in general, boys will have their adult voice by the age of 16. In the meantime, expect some ups and downs that may be out of your control. Here are some quick ideas to control the cracking, in case of an important speech or other communication needs in athletics, music, or other club activities. One, warm up! The first words after being silent for some time might be surprisingly high pitched. Clear the throat a bit and give some "hum"

noises before public speaking. Work from a low tone in your range to a few in the mid-range, a little like a vocalist might warm up to sing. This doesn't take much or draw too much attention your way—it can be done in just a few seconds without others really noticing. Another way to decrease vocal cracks is to keep enough air flowing through your throat as you speak. Use a bit more pressure as if speaking loudly or to a larger audience. Many breaks in the voice occur when that pressure trails off and you speak more quietly.

Even with those tips, there's no guarantee that you won't experience some cracking. One of your best ways to cope if that happens? A sense of humor! Learn to laugh at yourself—it goes a long way toward easing any embarrassment that might shine through if your voice breaks. A little chuckle and, *"Sorry about that. Take two!"* might be all it takes. Trying to hide the issue might not work, so come up with a few clever quips to let everyone know you're growing a great personality along with that great voice. Try, *"Oh, man! I crack myself up,"* or *"Breaking news here!"* If anyone ever becomes really bothersome, you can be direct but polite: *"Hey, be nice, please. My voice is just changing, that's all."* Smile and move on.

Sounds Good

In the end, your voice will be unique, just like the rest of you. Your manner of speech will be impacted by language, geographic location, family, and friends, but the tone will be all yours. It might be higher, lower, or different in inflection, which is the pitch and expression in how you pronounce words. Plenty of great speakers throughout history had uncommon voices, and plenty have managed speech impediments. What you do with your voice is the powerful part. You have the ability to build others up or bring others down with a simple turn of phrase. Be mindful of this going through adolescence—part of *growing up great* is to build mental and social health, too. And don't worry, in chapter 6 (page 95) we'll work on how to handle tough scenarios and how to manage your own emotions and respectfully respond to others.

BELOW THE BELT

Well, my friend, the time has come to discuss *those things*. You know, the parts of that nether region below the belt. We've already mentioned a few changes that occur "down there" during puberty, but you deserve to have all the details so you know how to remain healthy and safe in your journey through adolescence. A boy's external reproductive organs, called *genitals* or *genitalia*, include the main organ of the penis and the two round organs hanging below and behind the penis called the testes, or testicles. We will use these terms instead of the slew of slang words out there so we can remain polite and accurate.

Unlike the outward changes that might be observable by other people, genital changes will be personal and private. These will really only be seen and felt by you. In some ways, that's good! Every boy has the right to privacy with the growth of their reproductive organs. The primary sex characteristics that develop in the penis, testes, and related body parts are not public matters. There may be puberty topics that are covered in school or at home. Educationally speaking, not everything needs to remain secretive during your development. But you still might be left with a few of the more personal questions. That's why you've picked up this book. Curiosity is normal. And let's say it again: Knowledge is power. Learning about puberty changes will always be beneficial. So let's dive down into the depths of the genital region with common questions and necessary topics.

THE HAIR DOWN THERE

Pubic hair was discussed a bit in chapter 2 (page 17) when we examined hair care. We mentioned that pubic hair largely depends on genes and is generally the color of other body hair like eyebrows or underarm hair. No matter the color, type, or amount, keeping pubic hair clean and groomed will help you through puberty into adulthood. Like everything during puberty, boys will experience pubic hair growth differently. The pubic bone is that hard part beneath the skin between the belly button and the penis. You might start to see fine hairs begin on the sides of the pubic bone close to the crease of the thighs, or perhaps you'll notice coarse hair starts at the base of the penis near the body. You will also experience some sparse hairs sprouting on the scrotum, which is the sack of skin that contains the testicles. Pubic hair will be noticeable around age 12 and continue to fill in until age 17 or 18. Some hair underneath the testicles, on and under the buttocks, as well as on top of the tailbone, can also be common by adulthood.

Keep pubic hair clean by scrubbing in the shower at the same time that you wash other body hair. Pubic

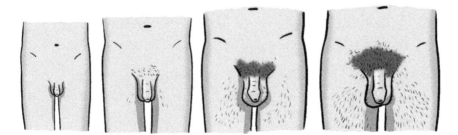

hair is generally curly and—often depending on race and heritage—is sometimes matted down closer to the skin compared to other body hair; make sure to get soap or shampoo close in toward the skin. Cleaning well will keep bacteria at a lower number, and this will prevent body odor. Cleanliness will also reduce the irritations at the pores that cause itchy skin. An old, common term for this is "jock itch." Jock itch is caused by a fungus. It often occurs in athletes because fungi thrive in a warm environment. Wet, sweaty skin that's covered with tight-fitting clothing can create the perfect storm for fungi to fester. A common sign of jock itch is an irritating rash on the genitals, inner thighs, and even the crack of the buttocks. Regularly cleaning the pubic hair will drastically reduce the risk of any rash.

Grooming pubic hair is exactly like we discussed with chest hair—by adulthood, some men choose to groom their pubic hair, while others leave it be. There are only a few reasons for this, most of which are simply personal preference. Trimming is rarely a physical necessity, by any means. If the pubic hairs get too long and are tangled or pulled by underwear, athletic cups, or other clothing, a quick snip with small body hair scissors will bring the length down and quickly do the trick. Otherwise, be careful of shaving because razor burn is more likely in the pubic region. Irritation can easily develop on the pubic bone, where the band of elastic underwear might press, or in warm places like the crease at the legs and scrotum where skin-to-skin contact is constant.

GENITAL CHANGES

The genitals will gain a little size at the beginning of puberty, but this gain might be unnoticeable. Significant change will generally be observable by age 13 or 14. However, things might slow a bit from time to time before gaining momentum to your adult body by age 18+. The testicles will enlarge first. Remember that testicles aren't so much "balls"—they are more oval in their shape.

The testicles begin their main function once hormones trigger them into action when puberty begins. The testes are responsible for creating sperm, which are the microscopic cells that contain a man's DNA. Remember from chapter 1 (page 1) that DNA contains the genetic code to make you who you are. The purpose of sperm cells is to contribute to reproduction, which is detailed a bit later in this chapter. The testes have attachments at the top called the epididymis, where mature sperm are temporarily held and small connecting tubes go up inside the body. The testicles will always be very sensitive, so take good care of your little guys. We'll discuss how in the upcoming sections.

Boys have a built-in protection system for the testes. The scrotum is the sac of skin that contains

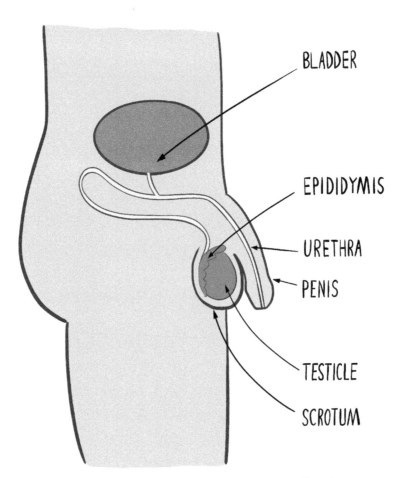

BLADDER

EPIDIDYMIS

URETHRA

PENIS

TESTICLE

SCROTUM

the testes and connected parts. This skin will enlarge and thicken by age 13 or 14, and all of the genitals might turn darker in skin tone over time. Sperm cells require a very specific temperature to develop properly. You may already know that the human body hovers around 98.6 degrees Fahrenheit. Well, human sperm production requires about 4 degrees lower than normal body temperature. This is why the testes are external, as opposed to the internal organs that females have for cell production. The skin of the scrotum can tighten to bring the testes up closer to the body for warmth or loosen to drop them down away from the body to cool off. This is human science, and you don't have to think about it at all—your body does it all on its own. You might particularly notice this when jumping in a cold swimming pool or relaxing in the sun on a warm, summer day. Keep that to yourself, though. No need to announce this marvel of nature.

As the testicles and scrotum gain size, the penis will follow in length and overall girth (thickness). Similar to the testes, the penis will mature in noticeable form around ages 12 to 13 and will be fully grown around ages 17 to 18. Perhaps the most common question with boys during puberty is, "Am I normal?" Concerns about penis size can happen just like those regarding any other changes with height, voice, or body hair. As long as everything is functional, and you remember that puberty changes can always differ between boys, rest assured that you are growing just fine. More details about the penis are discussed in the remaining sections of this chapter.

Boxers or Briefs?

"What underwear should I wear?" Such a common question! By asking, it means you care about yourself and your health. The quick answer? You choose. Boxers are looser and fit more like shorts, while briefs have bottom elastic around the legs and fit a bit more snugly. There are even boxer briefs, which provide

more length down the leg with a similar feeling of briefs. Often, young boys are dressed in briefs in their childhood but can then make their own choice as they age into puberty. As usual, try a few things to see what you like. Both might provide a hole through the middle to provide quick access for urination needs. You'll want to find a brand and fit that doesn't open too much and you fall through—the penis is sensitive, so underwear protects it from the irritating rub on rougher materials like jeans and other attire.

The more in-depth answer is that the health of your testicles leans closer to boxers on this one. We just mentioned how sperm cells require a very specific temperature to develop properly. For adult men who are looking to reproduce, the number of healthy sperm increases the likelihood of having a baby. Testes can overheat when a man wears tight underwear. If the testicles are several degrees warmer than they should be, they are not able to produce enough mature sperm, resulting in low sperm count. Boxers allow the scrotum to do its job.

This doesn't mean you should change your behavior right now. In the end, it does come down to preference. However, you should always be looking out for your future health. If you are a brief-wearing young man, one thing to consider would be to allow your testicles breathing room as much as you can. This might mean wearing loose fitting clothing when home and lounging around, and particularly overnight.

SHOULD I WEAR A CUP?

If you are an athlete, you'll notice a bunch of options for athletic support during both practice and games. You won't want things bouncing around while running, jumping, and performing all the other movements of your sport. Jockstraps are a bit of a thing of the past. These are worn with or without a protective cup, and the older designs always had a supportive front with an open back end. More likely, with newer designs you'll be able to use a boxer brief athletic supporter, with options to insert a cup depending on your sport needs. These have become more comfortable and often "wick" away sweat from the body, leaving the athlete feeling drier during activity. Some athletic supporters even include antimicrobial material to keep germs away. Athletic supporters are snug and smart for the testicles during intense movement. Protect yourself early on for testicular health in the long run.

What Are Erections?

During puberty, you may begin to experience more erections and different stages of erections in the penis. An erection is when the penis becomes hard and stands up and out from the body because it is filled with blood. A relaxed, "soft" state is known as a *flaccid* penis. Stimulated, or aroused, is an excited state known as an *erect* penis. Although a slang term is "boner," we will use the term erection, since, technically, there is no bone there. Erections are normal and can occur for no reason at all besides the fact that hormones are helping the body grow. They can also happen if you find yourself attracted to someone or you think about anything sexual. Erections are healthy, but that doesn't mean they are always timely.

A flaccid penis is the state of things for the majority of each day. That said, erections might happen for one reason or another. While this is natural, it could prove to be a concern because an erection is not something to be made noticeable in a public place. Ways to manage an erection in public are to 1) try to refocus on the current task, whether it be in school or at home, 2) attempt to quickly and privately sweep the penis upward toward the beltline of your pants, or 3) find a way to excuse yourself to the restroom to calm things down. For the most part, erections will go away in a matter of minutes, so it might just be a waiting game. Standing up from a seated position might make the situation more apparent to others.

Erections will certainly happen overnight throughout puberty and into adulthood. This is healthy and actually a part of your sleep cycle—blood flow increases and decreases throughout the body and the pubic area during deep sleep and dream sequences. A boy doesn't have to be dreaming of anything sexual to have an erection while sleeping, but they certainly can coincide with sex-related dreams. During this overnight process, the body might also release semen, the fluid that contains sperm cells, in what's called a nocturnal emission. These are also known as wet dreams. This is how your body handles the increase of the hormone testosterone. Wet dreams are healthy and normal but might range with each particular boy. Some boys might have frequent wet dreams each week or two; others might not have them more than a few times throughout puberty.

Semen is a white, clear-ish fluid that is thicker than urine. It is a protein-rich mixture to keep sperm cells alive. Semen will be released in small amounts—only around a teaspoon of total fluid—in waves of contracting pulses called *ejaculation*. Ejaculation for men will coincide with a pleasurable feeling, and is also referred to as an orgasm.

While this all may sound complicated, the great news is that these body functions happen on their own. Even though semen is released through the same tube as urine, a tube known as the urethra, the science of the body is such that little doorways called valves take care of things without you having to do any specific thinking. You won't urinate and ejaculate at the same time.

Purposefully causing yourself to have an erection and to ejaculate is known as masturbation. Masturbation is done alone and in private. It is a healthy way of knowing your own body by adulthood. There is nothing harmful in masturbation; however, your personal or religious beliefs might cause you to abstain, or to choose not to touch yourself. If you masturbate, do so in private, take care of the skin and tissue down there, and never let it interfere with other activities in life—socially, academically, or otherwise. Always maintain a healthy life balance.

Circumcision

With differences in people, naturally there will be differences in anatomy. This means that the way the genitalia look will be unique, with small variances for each boy. The *foreskin*—the outer layer of skin along the shaft of the penis and over the tip, or head, of the penis—is sometimes surgically removed. Depending on culture and religion, this might be done at birth or even a few years into life. This is called *circumcision*. Every boy is born with foreskin, and you can be clean and healthy whether circumcised or not.

If you are uncircumcised and have foreskin covering the head of your penis, make sure to gently pull that skin back in the shower to clean the areas underneath. If circumcised, the head of the penis will always be exposed, but still clean around the foreskin every day. Be careful of getting too much soap in there, and rinse it thoroughly, especially because of the sensitivity of the urethra—that tiny hole where urine comes out. Getting soap in the urethra will cause a burning sensation when you pee.

If there are other burning sensations, either while urinating or simply all of the time, and you haven't gotten soap in your urethra lately, make sure to check with your parents right away to schedule time to see the doctor. Infections can happen because of viruses and bacteria, and you want to make sure everything is going great down there.

Reproduction

Reproduction is the process where organisms make more of themselves. It is the act of a man and a woman creating new life. Puberty is a time when boys gain the ability to reproduce. Even though the penis and testicles continue to mature until the end of puberty, a boy's parts are functional for reproduction upon the start of puberty. This means that once sperm cells are being made, a boy can reproduce. While that's possible in adolescence, that doesn't mean a boy is ready for his own child yet, especially mentally and socially.

Smart choices always need to be made regarding relationships and sexual activity, or *sex*, which is when two people have close, intimate, naked contact. There are different types of sexual contact depending on gender and the individuals involved. Heterosexual intercourse refers to the insertion of a man's erect penis into a woman's vagina. Reproduction can occur this way. Once semen is released into a woman's body, sperm cells work as a large group to locate and penetrate the ovum, or egg cell, for fertilization (aka conception). These little tadpole-like swimmers have a long tail used for travel and a receptor on their nose that finds the ovum. Each sperm from a man carries half of his chromosomes with the DNA code for new life. The offspring (children) will replicate this DNA code as cells multiply within a woman's womb.

Erections and wet dreams are a healthy part of the puberty process because a boy's body is preparing for the future. Take care of the health of your reproductive system now, and be safe with sexual choices, so you can have options for a family of your own as an adult.

WACKY FACTS

Did you know the sperm cell is the smallest cell in the human body, male *or* female? Sperm measure around 50 microns in length. A micron is an abbreviation for micrometer, or a millionth of a meter. A micron is .00004 of an inch. Most of a sperm cell's length is the tail—the head of a sperm is only 5 microns across. There are anywhere between 50 million and 1 billion sperm cells released by a healthy adult man during ejaculation. These cells are so small, however, that they all fit into a single teaspoon of fluid.

Staying Safe and Self-Exams

Male genitalia is widely regarded as the most sensitive part of a boy's body. There are many nerve endings there, which is why both the testes and the penis are highly susceptible to pain if bumped or hit. It doesn't take much to drive pain into action. If hit in the genitals, time will be needed to gain your composure. If there is lingering pain, unusual swelling, or any major bleeding or bruising, check in with an emergency room immediately. This is why it is never a good idea to joke around with other boys by hitting or kicking them in the groin. Have respect for others as you would yourself. A hit to the genitals is a last resort to an immediate physical threat. Otherwise, don't risk damage to the reproductive system and find better ways to express friendship and humor. Everyone will be thankful.

Self-exams are a healthy way of knowing your own body and reducing the risk of disease. Communicable diseases are those that are contagious and can be spread, including sexually transmitted infections (STIs) that can be spread through sexual contact. Noncommunicable diseases are not spread from person to person. Being aware of yourself and your choices in combination with checking for changes can help prevent both. Testicular problems can be spotted early with self-exams. Use the following steps, best done in or after a warm shower.

STEP 1: Cup one testicle at a time using both hands.

STEP 2: Gently roll the testicle between the thumb and first finger, applying slight pressure.

STEP 3: Note the epididymis and attached tube (spermatic cord) at the back of the testicle.

STEP 4: Feel for lumps, changes in size, or anything else irregular.

While most of this chapter dealt with private matters, any time you have concerns regarding genital health, never wait or keep anything secret—make time to immediately reach out to a trusted adult. We will discuss how to do this in chapter 7 (page 111).

FEEDING AND FUELING YOUR BODY

Up to this point, we have covered all the major changes to the body that occur during puberty. It's pretty incredible how the human body grows and transitions through adolescence into adulthood. You are one amazing dude, dude. While a lot of puberty changes occur without any special action on your part, there are in fact some things you can do that will help. You deserve to know the three main habits that help boys remain healthy through it all—nutrition, exercise, and sleep. No secrets there, really, but each one can be neglected from time to time. So, what details should you understand for this trifecta of health? In this chapter, we will examine the ways to feel good and stay confident in your journey through puberty.

NUTRITION

The human body is like a well-oiled machine, my friend. You are a high-performance sports car. You have a turbo engine with automatic transmission. You have a top-of-the-line navigation system. You have automatic air-conditioning, safety features, and cruise control. Plus, you look good. But here's one of the best parts: Even with all those perks, you are still extraordinarily fuel-efficient.

This is more than just a fun analogy. Your body needs food just like any engine or machine might need fuel. In order to feel good and work well, we need to fuel up correctly and consistently throughout the week. Your diet is that fuel. A diet, defined simply, is the food you

eat. It's the kind of food you take in day after day. To have a diet doesn't necessarily mean restricting foods, as in eating less during a meal or consuming fewer calories overall. The term diet refers to the choices you make regarding food and what you put into your body for fuel.

For the most part, your parents have the ultimate say in what food comes in and out of your life. You might not be preparing your own meals, but there's a chance you get to add suggestions to the grocery list or help in other ways. If you pay attention now, you can feel informed and prepared once you are fully responsible for your own eating habits.

Calories and Nutrients

A calorie is a unit of energy in food. Consider calories the name for human fuel. Nutrients are substances in food that we need to grow and live. Calories come from three major nutrients, called macronutrients: carbohydrates, proteins, and fats. Carbohydrates include sugars and starches in food, and their primary function is to provide the body with energy. Carbohydrates, or carbs for short, also help the brain and digestive system work properly. Each gram of carbohydrate provides us with four calories.

Proteins are made up of building blocks called amino acids and provide the structure and maintenance of cells, tissues, and organs. Proteins also help with our muscles, blood, and immune system. Each gram of protein also provides us with four calories.

Dietary fats often get a bad reputation, but there are plenty of healthy fats in foods that our body needs each day. Fats are used to support cell growth, body warmth, vitamin absorption, and heart health. Each gram of fat provides us with nine calories, making fats a great backup source of energy.

Carbs, proteins, and fats are our calorie-providing macronutrients, and with help from vitamins, minerals, and the almighty water, our day-to-day tasks can be completed. We live long and we live healthy. Habits are actions that are regularly practiced. Dedicating time to developing healthy food habits now will make it easier to stay healthy through adolescence and into the rest of life. Part of *growing up great* means developing and maintaining self-respect, and a large part of self-respect is taking care of the body. That includes knowing and caring about what you put into yourself for food.

A Colorful Plate

The government and leading nutrition organizations have recommendations for healthy eating. Often, good food gets termed health*ful*, because it creates good health. People, on the other hand, are healthy because they can have good health and well-being. The idea of having healthful foods isn't to take the enjoyment out of eating. It is quite the opposite—having a healthful diet helps us feel great and keeps us functioning at our best.

First and foremost, always take into consideration any food allergies or other dietary requirements you might have such as vegetarianism or veganism (avoiding meat and/or all animal products). Recommendations from doctors and nutritionists need to be taken with personal beliefs and other needs in mind. Once that's done, find a variety of foods that you enjoy. Healthful eating does not have to mean forcing down food we hate or suffering through bland or boring meals. Food can taste good and can be good for us at the same time.

Instead of getting too caught up in numbers—serving size measurements and calories—food variety can be attained with a "colorful plate." A great goal is to try to make half of each meal fruits and vegetables. Another great goal is to find whole grains by choosing foods such as whole wheat bread, wheat pasta, wheat tortillas, and brown rice.

Check out some more basics on what a colorful plate might look like:

RED foods help the heart, the skin, and the immune system. Examples are apples, red peppers, watermelon, tomatoes, grapes, and strawberries.

ORANGE foods help the eyes, immune system, and circulatory system. Examples are oranges, carrots, sweet potatoes, orange peppers, peaches, and cantaloupe.

YELLOW foods help cell growth, vision, and heart health. Examples are lemons, papayas, corn, pineapple, yellow peppers, and mangos.

GREEN foods help with bone health, the immune system, and the reproductive system. Examples are spinach, avocados, broccoli, zucchini, lettuce, and green beans.

BLUE AND PURPLE foods help with tissue repair, the circulatory system, and disease control. Examples are blueberries, cabbage, plums, blackberries, eggplant, and prunes.

OTHERS In small amounts, and if you can stomach it, go with dairy like milk, yogurt, and cheese. Other options might be an alternative to cow's milk; some people enjoy almond milk. Find dairy varieties and/or alternatives with limited added sugars.

Use the Resources section (page 129) in the back of this book for more information on nutrition.

Sugar Highs and Getting Salty

We all know how sugar tastes. It's so good, right? No argument there. And salt is pretty tasty, too. But don't be that guy who argues that a colorful plate is one with red gummy worms, orange cheese balls, yellow French fries, and blue jelly beans—all washed down with a green soda. Nope. Nice try. Besides creating a colorful plate that is rich in fruits, vegetables, and whole grains, another solid goal for a healthy diet is to limit added sugars and unnecessary salt (the common word for sodium). In the short term, these might make us feel good. However, there is often a crash within a few hours after that initial sugar rush. We can feel dehydrated after a meal that was filled with sodium. Too much of each can affect your circulatory system and leave you feeling worse than before.

By adolescence you might be awarded more freedom and time with your friends. This means the potential to have more opportunities to eat fast food, buy junk food at school, or snack on something while out around town. Be careful of overindulging! Bad habits can form fast.

Aim for food that does not come prepackaged. This is a general rule of thumb, of course, but fresh, natural food is a healthier choice than products. Products come in bags and boxes—items like chips, candy, crackers, and even cereals. These tend to be processed, which means there are added sugars, salts, and other flavorings meant to change the taste for the better. Products are generally snack foods, desserts, and sodas, and the companies who make them might even add vitamins or brag about certain fruit ingredients to boost the marketing appeal. Even juice can come with added sugar. For example, an apple is an excellent source of carbohydrates, containing natural sugars that the body can use. Apple juice, however, can contain as much sugar as soda.

Cheer up, pal. Limiting additives and processed foods doesn't mean you can never have treats. Realize snacks and desserts are just that—they are treats meant for small quantities. Snack food won't make for a full meal, and desserts aren't needed every day. The brain and other body organs know that eating a meal itself should in fact be enjoyable. Humans have evolved to find the actions of chewing and swallowing as important parts of the eating process for both the body and the mind. In addition, meals are great social gatherings where we can hang out with family and friends to communicate all our great thoughts, feelings, and emotions. Our bodies are made to crave the stuff that best sustains our energy needs, which is why real food usually wins the battle against snacks or supplements like drinks, powders, and pills meant to help with nutrients. Once you recognize food as the fuel for your body systems, you can notice the benefits of healthy eating while still enjoying each meal. Avoid checking the fridge or cupboard when you're bored. Instead, be a good helper as your family makes its meals and find a different activity instead of raiding the kitchen. Need ideas? See the next section about exercise.

EATING WITH ALLERGIES (AND OTHER ISSUES)

It is common to have allergies to food. By now, you and your family have checked with the doctor to figure out if you have any allergic reactions to food. These can range from peanut and tree nut allergies, to dairy or lactose intolerance, to issues with shellfish. There are many other allergies as well. Sometimes, people can outgrow food allergies; other times they maintain a diet that avoids foods or ingredients that trigger a reaction. You can stay positive and confident when eating differently from others by being open and honest. It is helpful for friends to know your allergies. If you get asked if you'd like an allergy-inducing food, reply with something simple and honest like, "I appreciate it, but I'm actually allergic. What are my other options?" Some people might have questions for you, but you can just stick to the facts. It causes a reaction, and it's something you need to avoid. Be strict in your habits about checking food labels for your allergens and come to learn which common foods or products would be an issue. If you have a vegetarian diet or other special dietary needs and will be out to dinner or at a party, it would be helpful to let any adults know ahead of time so they can accommodate your needs.

EXERCISE

One of the greatest ways to help manage your body as you grow through puberty is to stay physically active. Active kids become active teens, and active teens become active adults. It's a habit that is natural for any child—we all know how kids love to run and jump and play. By now in your life you have found some things you enjoy that are physical, but don't rule out new opportunities. You might find a new activity that is fun and challenging.

Physical activity has lots of benefits to a growing body. Regular exercise promotes health and physical fitness by maintaining muscle, balancing body fat, and strengthening bones. Physical activity also improves brain health by helping with memory, mood, and academic performance in school. Exercise helps prevent disease and is a large part of social connection during adolescence. Friends are made and kept through sports and outdoor play. During puberty, active time provides oxygen to the brain to help the hormones do their job. Activity gets blood flow to the extremities so your body can develop and work through growing pains. Movement also stabilizes stress and emotions. As you can tell, there are so many reasons to get active every day!

One final reason to get moving is to help with sleep. We are able to get to sleep faster and have deeper, regenerating sleep because of physical activity—even movement from earlier in the day. In a later section of this chapter we will highlight the function of sleep and the sleep needs of a boy going through puberty.

The recommendation is for adolescents to get 60 minutes of physical activity a day. This can be all at once or it can be cumulative (over the span of a few hours), but it doesn't have to stop at an hour. Physical activity should be intense enough to get the heart rate up to where, if you pause and reflect for a few seconds, you can feel your heart beating in your chest. There are specific heart rate checks to see if you are moving at a good intensity; if you're interested, website links can be found in the Resources section in the back of the book (page 129).

Athletes

Do you consider yourself an athlete? Or maybe you simply love sports and activity. You don't have to be the best at what you do to consider yourself athletic. Also, athleticism can develop with practice, which you undoubtedly know. That's the cool part about human movement. With strength, conditioning, and

skill work, anyone can improve at their chosen activity. Athleticism in one sport often transfers over to other activities. Things like coordination, speed, and agility can help no matter what athletic endeavor you attempt. Be open to the possibility that what you excelled at as a young kid might not be what you can excel at as a teenager. Cross-training also develops overall physical skills, so giving multiple sports a try can be a good idea throughout each year. And be coachable! If you want to improve at your sport, you will benefit by being able to listen and apply what you've been shown. Failure isn't permanent; it is a chance to learn and adapt.

Depending on the sport, you may need specific equipment, apparel, or safety gear. This can range from simple workout clothing to athletic underwear, like we detailed in chapter 4 (page 66). Besides a cup or athletic supporter, other items to consider would depend on your sport. You might need shoes or cleats; a mouthguard; a helmet; athletic tape; knee, elbow, or other body pads; and, depending on vision needs, sports goggles.

Nonathletes

Active time does not need to include organized sport. One of the greatest ways to get moving is to simply create fun outdoor games with friends. Public parks, playgrounds, and indoor gyms are sometimes available in the community. Other options are to find an open field or neighbor's yard to throw or kick a ball around, play a hide-and-seek or capture-the-flag type of game, or create a tough little obstacle course. You could even race to various places around your neighborhood (staying safe around roads, of course). Maybe music is more your thing. Alone or with friends, you could always put on some of your favorite music and get moving. You don't have to consider yourself a good dancer—just start bouncing around. Maybe this takes you on a run, maybe it lets you climb a tree, or maybe it just feels goofy in a good way and you let yourself get some energy out. Mind your manners with family and anyone else nearby, though. Your favorite beats shouldn't stop you from being a respectful young man.

SLEEP

The final piece of the healthy trio of self-care is possibly the most important. Sleep is not for the weak. Sleep is for the strong and the smart. It's for the motivated and the successful. It's for the athlete, the musician, the artist, the writer, and the techie. It's for everyone who cares about their well-being. Sleep is non-negotiable. What this means is that sleep has no substitutions. No exceptions. For instance, there is no nap that can take the place of a good night's sleep. There is also no catching up on sleep on the weekends. You can't sleep for 5 hours one night and 12 hours the next and expect to feel good—you won't make up for lost time. You can't

pool it up like a piggy bank, and you can't write IOUs once you're in debt. Either you get the sleep you need for the day, or you don't.

During sleep, the body and brain recover from the day. Not only this, but there are a series of natural body responses that occur during the night of rest. Maintenance repair occurs with both your muscle cells and connecting tissues. Your brain and central nervous system work to consolidate, or file together, memory and learning. There are multiple hormone responses during sleep that trigger growth, especially during puberty. You might notice yourself feeling more tired than usual through puberty. Your body is using a lot of energy. You want to get the most from your body, right? Then sleep must be a priority.

POWER IN NUMBERS

Eighty-five percent of teenagers are sleeping less than the recommended 8–10 hours per night. More than 90 percent of teenagers use some form of technology in the hour before bedtime. The issue with this is exposure to light from a screen or digital device can delay the correct hormone response to start sleep. If you have issues with your sleep, you are not alone! Nearly 17 percent of teens qualify for clinical diagnosis of insomnia (trouble falling asleep at night). To help, limit sugar, caffeine, and screen time throughout the day and definitely right before bed. If you have any sleep concerns, check in with your family doctor.

All this considered, being smart with sleep management does not mean a boy lacks drive or is missing out on anything. Too much work and a lack of recovery are actually a horrible combination for your health. While it may sound tough or feel self-assuring to say you worked so hard that you didn't sleep at night, that kind of behavior just leads to eventual shutdown. A balance of work and sleep is key. School and hobbies are necessary, but so is down time and rest. Sleep helps every aspect of life, including physical, mental, and social well-being.

Sleep Needs

So we've established that sleep is an absolutely essential part of everyday life. But how much should you shoot for? While sleep requirements vary from person to person, most adolescents need between 8 and 10 hours of sleep per night to function at their best. Boys going through puberty will feel great aiming for 9. A little more or a little less will depend on your age, your unique brain and body, as well as your activity level each day. At age 9, you may be better closing in on 11 hours each night. By age 18, you might work well at 8.5 hours. What is certain is that you cannot sidestep your sleep needs. Get that shut-eye!

The average adolescent sleeps only 7 hours per night. In today's fast-paced society, 7 hours of sleep may sound pretty good. In reality, though, it might be a recipe for constant sleep loss, also known as chronic sleep deprivation. Being sleep deprived means a person gets insufficient sleep, leading to health issues. Even lacking just an hour every day can cause you to be more irritable and impulsive. It can cause safety issues as well.

You may not be noticeably sleepy the next day, but even slightly less sleep can affect your reaction time, your ability to fight off infections like colds and flus, and your performance in school assignments, athletics, and musicianship. Achieving the right amount of sleep each night will help you stay alert, help you problem solve, and even help your self-confidence. The best way to feel good through puberty and into adulthood is to go to sleep at the same time every night and wake up around the same time every morning, no matter what day of the week.

If you have difficulty falling asleep, don't watch the clock. Don't even count sheep. You can help things by limiting sugar, caffeine, late-night exercise, and screen time before bed. And while on the pillow, focus on one positive thought, and one thought only. Letting the mind wander might sound like a good way to drift to sleep—in actuality, that keeps the brain awake. While slowing your breathing, think about one good thing that happened that day, or one thing coming up you're excited about. And, while we're on the topic, keep in mind that almost everyone will have nightmares. Scary dreams are part of the brain's defense mechanism to learn and avoid threats. While they aren't completely avoidable, you can limit nightmares with consistent sleep habits and by controlling stress and anxiety. Chapter 6 (page 95) will examine emotions more in depth.

WACKY FACTS

Calories aren't all equal in terms of the volume of food. 100 calories of broccoli will fill up a large bowl; 100 calories of cheese looks like 4 small dice.

Exercise isn't just for your body. Working out sharpens your memory, too. Regular exercise is a brain boost—it stimulates the creation of new neurons (brain cells) and helps us perform better on mental activities.

Sleep isn't only about resting. Because of all the repair going on overnight, sleeping actually burns more calories than watching television.

FEELINGS AND FRIENDS

We've established that puberty is a time of physical growth. But in reality, life is much more than that. The journey through adolescence includes other changes, not just those within the body. Typically, we can classify life, and therefore health, into three main categories: physical well-being, mental well-being, and social well-being. From there, things can get as detailed as needed. For instance, parts of life like environmental health, spiritual health, and emotional health might become increasingly important. But the health triangle is a good place to begin the process of understanding ourselves. Throughout this book, we have taken a big dive into the physical aspects of puberty. Let's make sure we cover mental and social health, too.

MOOD SWINGS AND MORE

In the first chapter, we mentioned that your growth through puberty is prompted by hormones. Remember, hormones are chemicals released in the body, sort of like messengers. They control and coordinate functions of your internal organs without you having to even think about things. Hormones are secreted by a system in the body called the endocrine system, which includes a very important section of the brain called the pituitary gland. During puberty, the pituitary gland helps with your physical growth and all the changes described in earlier chapters, but it causes your emotions to change as well. Just like your body is adjusting to all the new hormones during puberty, so is your mind.

Because of these hormonal changes, you might feel ups and downs in your emotions that are often called mood swings. These are the waves of emotions in your journey as you grow up, and they can create a rocky ride. Hang in there, Captain. One moment you might be happy, and the next you might feel sad for no apparent reason. You might swing from being angry and yelling to hurt and crying. This can be confusing, but the first thing to understand is that there's nothing wrong with this. Hormones will sort themselves out through puberty; in the meantime, prepare for the fact that you might become overly sensitive, irritable, jealous, or withdrawn from friends and family. You might also feel giddy and hyper out of nowhere or feel overwhelmingly silly at inappropriate times.

Check out the next few sections for coping skills.

Mindfulness

There are some things you can do to help manage mood swings. First things first: In a moment of intense emotion, take a step back and try to view your own life with a different lens. Try to see what is happening as if you are looking in on yourself like a movie. This is difficult to do, particularly in times of frustration and annoyance. But if you can acknowledge your current feelings at any given time, this is known as mindfulness.

To be mindful means to live in the present moment. It means you are aware of your "here and now" without dwelling on the past or worrying about the future. It also means you recognize your environment, like your school environment, your bedroom environment, or your social environment and other people in your surroundings. Being mindful of your environment can help you determine how to manage your emotions because you can consider the consequences of your behavior in each unique situation. If you create an outburst of yelling and screaming at your friend's house, how will that make you look? If you are arguing back and forth with a parent in public, is that the attention you really want?

Finally, being mindful involves naming your feelings without self-judgment. If you feel mad and annoyed, then feel mad. If you are sad and bummed out, then be sad. Reacting to feelings is something we can't control. It happens first and fast, and within a few seconds to minutes of our life experiences. Responding to feelings, on the other hand, allows processing time to see our emotions playing out like the scenes of a movie. If you can focus on the present moment, consider the environment, and recognize your feelings, you are then able to respond to life events.

Coping Skills

Other coping skills that can help with mood swings and stress management are the essential brain activities in the list on the following pages.

FOCUS TIME: Set goals and challenges.

EXAMPLES: Brainstorm hopes for the week; find inspirational quotes; list the pros and cons for an upcoming decision; write down your strengths; identify a few weaknesses; create a plan of action for the next month.

CREATIVE TIME: Be spontaneous and creative.

EXAMPLES: Write; draw; paint; sing; dance; act; take photographs; play a musical instrument; make up a game to play with friends.

SOCIAL TIME: Social time with others.

EXAMPLES: Use humor with friends; talk to someone you trust; write a note to someone you care about; spend unstructured time with friends or family; care for or play with a pet.

ACTIVE TIME: Movement strengthens the mind.

EXAMPLES: Exercise or play outside; practice a sport; stretch; take a walk; do some yard work; play a board game that involves laughter or movement.

DOWN TIME: Relax and decompress with music, movies, or games.

EXAMPLES: Listen to music; take a quick, 30-minute screen break for your favorite show or video game; play a board game; watch a movie on a night you don't have homework. Limit to 90-120 minutes a day.

INWARD TIME: Quiet reflection helps set future expectations.

EXAMPLES: Read; pray or meditate; clean or organize a part of your room in silence; take a warm shower; daydream while on your bed or outside.

SLEEP TIME: Recover from the day and consolidate experiences for learning.

EXAMPLES: Focus on breathing before bed; plan the exact time for "lights out"; keep a calendar of how many days in a row you achieve 9+ hours of sleep.

Sharing is Caring

Everyone has their own things going on. If you ever feel overwhelmed with emotions or experience social situations that are frustrating, keep this in mind. You are not the only one. The tricky thing, however, is to realize you won't necessarily see or hear about other boys dealing with mental and social challenges. Moods, friendships, and attractions are mostly in the brain. Sure, our thoughts, feelings, and emotions are relayed into actions, but much of that is unseen. You won't be able to see every detail of another person's life, and vice versa. They won't be able to know exactly what's going on with you.

If you're confused by emotions, or your mood swings seem out of balance, communication helps. It's fine to keep some things to yourself. You deserve privacy, after all, and not just with your physical changes. You might enjoy some more quiet, personal time, but know when to reach out if anything feels like it's out of the ordinary or your emotions are out of your control. Open the lines of communication with a parent or a trusted adult. They are on your side and will be willing to listen. Sometimes, just a listening ear is all we need. For other times, seek out an expert to best guide you. Remember, talking through emotions can be helpful. This is in fact the "manly" thing to do—after all, you are trying to understand your feelings in order to be your best self. This self-respect transfers into social interactions, so communication is a big part of *growing up great*.

The Resource section (page 129) in the back of the book can help! Be sure to check it out at some point, and, as always, refer to a doctor in person for further help.

WACKY FACTS

Lots of things can affect our mood: the type of food we eat, time indoors or outdoors, a clean or cluttered bedroom, technology time, and even our dreams. Did you know that color can affect changes in mood? For instance, blue can cause feelings of peace and calmness, red is linked with warmth and comfort, and green generates feelings of health and good luck.

FRIENDSHIPS IN FLUX

It's okay to wonder if your friend group is right for you. Friendships through adolescence can change, and that's because people can change! Change isn't something to fear. People are allowed to grow up and become a different person, and that includes you and your choice in friends as you age.

By the end of elementary school and into your middle and high school years, interests can change drastically. What you enjoy in fifth grade will not be the same as what you enjoy in eighth grade, which will not be the same as in your senior year of high school. Interests in sports, extracurricular activities, hobbies, and even subjects in school can all vary from your friends. This means that friend groups will change. That's normal, and it can actually be exciting to keep the old friends you have and hang out with the new friends you are making.

Communication Is Key

One way to keep up with everyone is by communicating both in person and in text, either through the phone or the Internet. Even if a friend moves and you no longer live close to each other, our world of technology makes it possible to still talk from time to time. If you find yourself disagreeing with friends, however, or having repeated arguments, do a mindfulness check to see the big picture. Is there an issue because of a certain circumstance? Most likely, things can be smoothed over. Or is it more serious, and you need to be open and honest with a friend? If you need to make the tough decision to change who you're spending time with, communication is still powerful. Simply state that you have chosen to hang out with a different friend. That's respectful, and it's especially self-respectful if a so-called friend pressures you to do something you're not comfortable doing. A true friend won't force you into any scenario that compromises your integrity, which is the beliefs and morals that you have in life.

If you find yourself falling out of a friendship that you do want to keep, that can certainly cause hurt feelings. Again, communication is key. Try to be direct in questioning what is going on and if things can improve. You can always seek out a trusted adult for additional help. In the end, it might be an unfortunate truth that you're both better off moving on without each other. That said, kindness always wins, buddy. Be respectful even if parting paths.

POWER IN NUMBERS

At times, finding friends can be natural and occurs without much work, while at other times it requires us to reach out to socialize. Here are some friendship memories from a few men who have been in your shoes.

"As a kid, I moved all the time and was faced with the task of making new friends. One common bond was sports and hobbies. Those interests helped develop friendships that I still value to this day."
– Kris L.

"Around age 12, I first connected with groups outside of my core childhood friend group. I found myself with different friend groups, all with various interests, and it was cool to have that experience. By being myself and sticking to what I enjoyed doing, new friends fell into place."
– Jeff B.

"When I moved, I learned that anyone who was willing to talk to me, the new kid, was a possible friend. This made me pretty open to everyone and allowed me to become friends with all sorts of kids—I didn't have a group or a clique, really. I was often a bridge between different types of people. This comes in handy and stays with you as an adult."
– Kapil K.

You're in Control

The great news is that you're always the captain of your journey, which puts you in control of your crew. No, dude, you can't control other humans, of course. What this means is that you can always choose your friends. Based on positive personality characteristics, you control who you hang around. Think about what you value in another person who you might be spending time with. These might be things like trust, a sense of humor, reliability, honesty, or empathy, which is understanding another person's feelings because of similar experiences. Finding your crew might be tough at times and smooth sailing at others, but it'll always be worth it to have friends to lean on as you all journey through adolescence.

MORE THAN JUST FRIENDS

Depending on your current age, you might be interested in relationships with other people that develop into more than just a friendship. It is natural to find an attraction to others, particularly in the later stages of puberty. Some boys might not develop an attraction or a deep connection to another person, while others might try dating when the time feels right. Even though some pieces of attraction might occur without much thought, ultimately this is another choice in life that is all yours. You have the final say in what, and who, you are or are not interested in for a relationship.

There are several ways to feel attraction. It could develop as a mental attraction, emotional attraction, or physical attraction. You might find interest in another person because you value their ideas or because you share common hobbies. You might think they are good looking or have nice facial features. You might share similar feelings or enjoy connecting in other close ways. It will take time to figure all of this out. You may not know enough about a person until you have had nearly daily interaction with them for months. Even then, there is no reason to rush into things.

Consent

You should never feel pressured to enter a relationship that you don't want. If that's the case, have the self-respect to set up boundaries and consent. Consent is the permission for something to happen. In a relationship, consent involves both individuals agreeing upon the same thing. Consent is the basis for anything physical and emotional that might develop between you and another person. For instance, if a friend tells you that you should date or go out with a specific person, you don't have to agree if it doesn't feel right. If a person you're dating wants to hold hands or kiss and you're not ready, it isn't something you have to do. Likewise, consent means you don't pressure someone else into anything, either. Never assume you can make physical contact. Listen to what the other person is expressing. If there isn't a clear, expressed agreement, the answer is "no." Your body is your own, and the same is true for other people—they have the final decision in what they are willing to do. Even if something occurred in the past, in a consensual relationship it doesn't have to happen again. Consent is respect. Clear communication is the main part of that.

More information on consent can be found in the Resources section (page 129).

Should I Say Something?

Parents might have input on your dating life and whether it is or isn't allowed. On the flip side of that, sometimes friends and family members give boys a hard time about crushes and dating interests. They might joke with you about possibilities, which is mostly just harmless teasing. It might get a little annoying, sure, but if it's simple and fun, you can just roll with it. Maybe even dish out a little sarcasm in return. ("*Am I ready for dates? Like, those things you eat? Not hungry but thank you!"*) In any event, be warned: People might bug you about asking out that certain someone.

Being brave and putting yourself "out there" to a person you like can end great . . . or it can end in rejection. It takes guts to communicate a crush to someone, but you should know going into it that your feelings might not be reciprocated. One way to handle this is to wait for the relationship to develop naturally. In the meantime, you can learn more about that person and their own feelings for you. Holding on to this secret can also be difficult, though, so you might choose to let them know instead. It might change the friendship, or it might not. You might date and stay together, or you might not. That's how these things work. Each crush or attraction is unique. You can always just recommend hanging out together. If you truly like them, that's what you want anyway—more time in activities you both enjoy. Whether or not you express your interest, if your feelings are honest and true, you'll know the right decision when the time comes.

FAMILY AND OTHER SAFE SPACES

As we complete our exploration of puberty and what it means to keep *growing up great*, it's important to note that even while you're in command—the captain of your own journey through adolescence—there is always a support crew in place.

A balance exists in our lives between our desire to be private and our desire to be public. Whether in adolescence or adulthood, people generally bounce back and forth between social time and alone time. It will be good for you to know what is healthy and appropriate with both.

Boys going through puberty deserve their privacy, as we've already mentioned, but boys also deserve to know that they're not alone. If need be, there are people who care and can help. Besides your friends, there's another support group to mention—your family and other trusted adults.

Here's what you can do to maintain a balance between privacy and public relationships, especially in this time of transition.

FIND A FRIENDLY EAR

Every boy needs to know where to go to find wisdom and remain safe. Books, websites, and other resources can be useful tools for gaining information. Yet, they are only tools. Most often, to gain the best support or the most accurate information during puberty, you need a real person. And the best person for that job? Someone who has been through it all. Because of this, the best resource is not a fellow classmate or a friend your age. You can plan on leaning on your friends

with some of the feelings you share or a few common changes you might be going through during puberty. However, if and when you have bigger questions or concerns, your best bet is an older family member or other trusted adult.

Who is a trusted adult in your life? That's for you to decide. This could be a parent, a relative, a family friend, a teacher, a coach, a doctor, or a school nurse—you might even know more than one such person. The key ingredient here is that they are trustworthy. They have known you and you have known them for enough time to develop a relationship where you are comfortable asking for help. It might be a quick question or it might be a more personal conversation that takes place. It might be fairly easy to do or it might be slightly embarrassing to reach out. Nonetheless, this person can and will help. Keep in mind this isn't someone who will keep secrets. It is someone who will tell you what you deserve to know or help with resources as needed.

Don't overthink things—communication on your end just needs to be something simple. To start, just ask! A private conversation is probably what you'd be looking for, so use something like, *"Hey, I was just wondering if I could run a question past you when you have a few private minutes?"* By using the word *private* this adult in your life will know it's something personal and at that point should be able to set aside some time. If not, they will at least tell you a better place for you to chat. Adults understand the potential stress of puberty, so don't worry about being awkward. Remain direct in your questions or needs and be yourself. Adults are just grown-up kids, my friend.

YOUR RIGHT TO PRIVACY

Let's state something strangely confusing about family members. They can be the most annoying people on Earth. But, when it comes down to it, these are the same people who you would do anything for. And they'd do anything for you. If you are honest with yourself, you know this is true. Depending on your circumstances, they are your blood, or they have become your blood. It's a balance, remember. It's okay to be private, but don't shut out the people who love you most.

There have been a few recurring themes in this book. Knowledge is power. *Growing up great* is self-respect. And, in recent chapters, communication is key. Once again, keep the lines of communication open with family members so they know you value your time alone. Through puberty, the waves of hormones will affect your physical and emotional changes, and it might be true that you find yourself wanting more down time without anyone else around. A good book, a game, a movie, your favorite song, or even just a daydream might feel like the perfect way to unwind. You have the right to some time alone. But make it clear to your parents and other family members what's going on, and, most importantly, that you'll be back after a quick reset. A break of 20 to 30 minutes might be all it takes. Be kind with how you explain this to those in your household. It's part of being a young man, but it also makes it more likely that they will respect your private time.

Another piece to privacy is what we discussed in the previous chapter: consent. As a reminder, consent means agreeing for something to happen. Consensual living is another great way to practice respect. In this instance, consent also means self-respect. You are in charge of your own body. You decide if and when anyone else gets to touch you. Again, being polite with family members is best. Hugs and kisses from relatives are often expected, but consensual touch in any relationship is always your call. If you're not comfortable with something, honesty and kindness go hand in hand. It is perfectly acceptable to say something like, *"Sorry, I am more comfortable right now with just a side hug."* Or maybe you'd rather state, *"Not feeling up to a hug right now. Fist bump okay? Thanks."* If someone crosses the line in any way that makes you feel uncomfortable, seek out your trusted adult immediately and let them know. No secrets, because that's not fair, and that's not safe.

For more information on this, check the Resources section (page 129) in the back of this book.

LOCKER ROOM STRATEGIES

One day you might find yourself in a public locker room needing to change clothes without any privacy stalls—a swimming pool, a camping or sporting event, or a school physical education setting. If this is the case, you can still create your own privacy and deal with any nerves regarding changing in public.

First, don't panic. If you are a little embarrassed about anything, keep in mind that no one is really looking. It may feel like you're on display, but in reality, everyone else is just doing their own thing. Next, a quick-and-easy changing method is in fact possible. Have your new clothes or swimsuit set out for an easy grab. Keep your shirt on as you change shorts or pants to allow for some coverage down below. Bend down a bit, or even face backward to the crowd if you choose. Finally, change the top half of your body, again with the new clothing ready at hand.

If you need to shower in a place without a lot of privacy, have the towel handy nearby for a fast in-and-out. Turning your back is a little help here, as are your hands if needed. Eyes down, if it feels better. Don't draw too much attention to yourself with conversations, but otherwise just be natural. Wash, change, and you're good to go.

PEER PRESSURE

Remember the health triangle from chapter 6 (page 95)? Social health is one of those essential parts. Managing your well-being with social interactions will keep your emotions in check, which can prevent stress from harming your physical health as well.

Just as boys develop at different rates through the physical changes of puberty, they develop at different rates socially, too. In terms of social life, you may develop new interests during adolescence, or you may not. You may develop new relationships or attractions during puberty, or you may not. Sports, music, and other hobbies might remain as priorities in life, but you might also notice them shifting a bit. It is quite possible you will notice the focus of your peers shifting as well. Known or unknown, this change in others can cause a change within you. Sometimes the pressure to be in with the cool crowd overrides common sense.

You've heard the phrase, "Everyone's doing it." The issue with this is that it's based on perception. Instead of reality, your *perception* might be "everyone's doing it." There's a difference. The bad news? Perception becomes reality. By simply thinking you're the only one not involved, even if those aren't the facts, then your behavior changes. If you think everyone is staying up late to play an online game, if you think everyone is vaping or using alcohol, if you think everyone is in a sexual relationship, then those perceptions can change your actual choices. Fear of missing out can drive adolescents to take avoidable risks. Instead of trusting any sneaky perceptions, focus on the truths: The majority of kids and teens are *not* using alcohol, are *not* using tobacco products, and are *not* inappropriately sexual online or in dating relationships. As it turns out, no, not everyone is doing it.

Great news: You already have the skills to stand up to peer pressure. By suggesting a different activity, changing the subject, or simply saying no, you are building your repertoire. You are *growing up great*. Realize this, too: Anyone who pushes you to do something you aren't comfortable with is not a real friend. Real friends are supportive. Real friends care.

You can help yourself by being mindful of your environment—where and with whom you're hanging out. Over time, you'll learn which situations to avoid. Sometimes, you only figure this out in the moment. As you age and change with puberty, you might find you are given more freedom with your free time. You also might find that people's expectations of you change. Depending on your growth, others might expect more from a boy who looks older than he is. You might even be confronted in a bullying scenario.

With all of these pressures piling up, it's possible to feel overwhelmed. At that point, you can stay safe by first defusing the situation and then removing yourself from the scene altogether. If needed, use an excuse. Funny as it sounds, putting the blame on parents can actually help. Try, *"I have to get home to make sure I'm not grounded."* Or, if you are offered something unsafe and don't have a way out for a few minutes, say, *"No thanks, I gotta get home soon anyway."* If it's an intimidation or a bullying situation, you can dodge a verbal or physical fight by being direct. *"Look, I don't want to fight. I'm just gonna leave."* You'll probably need to ignore insults from there. Not easy to do. Keep your cool by focusing on finding an exit strategy—fast. It is always smart to have a trusted adult just a phone call away. Upon reflection, you two can then brainstorm ways to keep you safe and avoid further confrontations.

STAYING SAFE (AND SANE) ON SOCIAL MEDIA

You know what's impressive? The expanding world of the Internet. You know what's scary? The expanding world of the Internet. Yep, the World Wide Web, and all of the various social media options, can be both helpful and hurtful. Like a few other things in life, it all depends on its use.

We've established that a healthy balance helps throughout puberty, and that includes nutrition, exercise, and sleep. We should also add screens to that mix. To maintain physical, mental, and social well-being in adolescence and into adulthood, your habits with screen time matter. Technology like TV, the Internet, and video games should be limited to one or two hours a day. The social media part of this equation is a bit tricky, since social pressures might make it feel like a necessity as a boy enters teenage years. Add in clever marketing from big-name companies, and that's a recipe for temptation that no developing brain can avoid.

First of all, it's okay if you are *not* on social media. Just like the previous section on peer pressure, it will only be your perception if you think everyone else is on there. Communicating face-to-face, in person, is our human default; not only is it natural, but it has also been crucial to our social development. Think of media on the Internet as an extension of that. When used correctly and appropriately, it can be a fun way to keep up with friends. It can also widen your world view, since we get to be connected to people with similar interests from potentially all over the world. That's definitely cool.

The opposite effect of social media is it can leave boys feeling *less* social, believe it or not. Feeling left out is a big downfall of the rise of social media in adolescents. Posts and check-ins can cause boys to think they're missing out. However, images and video of people online are not always what they appear to be. Think of media like a highlight reel of life, with all the great times and fun activities posted, and all the dull and mundane stuff left out. Plus, with photo filters, what you see might not actually be real.

There are some things to consider, if and when you choose to be on any social media outlets. What you

say or do on the Internet is forever. It may seem like deleted texts or photos are completely gone, or private browsing tabs can hide your personal information, but the truth is all of that might still be traceable. Not only can people screenshot almost anything with the click of a button, but your phone and computer have an invisible "address" on the Internet that can lead back to you. That's not to scare you. That's to let you know the truth. Knowledge is power, my dude.

One final note on Internet safety is a good reminder whether in real life or online: How would you like the world to view you? Think about who you want to be.

Then, be that person! Sending suggestive photos might be regrettable and is certainly not safe, particularly if communicating with strangers. And sending sexual pictures or texts, known as *sexting*, is also a slippery slope to scary repercussions you'd probably like to stay away from. Not only could that be inappropriate or embarrassing, but it might be illegal as well. Stay safe, and sane, by representing yourself on the screen as you would in any other situation. Remember that who you are online is not separate from who you are in person. Real life includes the Internet and social media, and you'll benefit if you treat them with respect. Your unique persona can still come through—just be genuine. Be the kind and respectful young man you are.

WACKY FACTS

Did you know a triangle is widely considered the strongest geometric shape? Triangles are very hard to distort from their normal shape because of their ability to distribute force evenly to the other sides. Similarly, our physical health, mental health, and social health are all equal in importance. But they also depend on each other. That life triangle you have built up through childhood helps you remain strong and healthy through adolescence. And keeping a great balance in your journey through adolescence sets you up for success in adulthood.

CONCLUSION

Well, my friend, our time together has come to an end. Your voyage across the ocean of adolescence is underway while this, your navigational guide, is always at hand. Time is like the wind at your back, pushing you in the right direction. You are equipped with the sails of genetics and the guiding rudders of healthy choices. It is going to happen, by golly—come rain or shine, in calm or high water. You are going to keep your life afloat through the growth and changes, and you'll come out a changed man.

Keep in mind that all of the water in the ocean can never sink a ship unless it gets *inside* a ship. Likewise, any negative things you encounter in life will never bring you down unless you let them get inside of you. Remember all of the changes and challenges we've covered in these chapters? They will be the *reasons* you *grow up great*. With the bombarding waters of puberty, you will remain resilient because that's what you were built to do. The safest place for a ship may be in the harbor, but that's not where you are meant to stay.

Promise me this, Captain: You will never let any setbacks get inside your head. You will stand proud through any storms. And you will remain a self-respecting person ready to pass on positivity to the next captain in line.

Aye, aye, dude?

GLOSSARY

Acne: inflamed pores that lead to bumps on the skin.

Adam's apple: the larynx, or voice box, with an outer wall of cartilage that is located in the middle of the throat.

Adolescence: the time between the beginning of puberty and adulthood.

Calorie: a unit of energy found in food.

Circumcision: the surgical removal of the foreskin around the head of the penis.

Consent: the permission for something to happen.

Ejaculation: contracting pulses where semen, the fluid containing sperm cells, is released. Coincides with a pleasurable feeling, and is also referred to as an orgasm.

Environment: the sum total of a person's surroundings.

Erection: an enlarged state of the penis where it becomes hard and stands up and out from the body because it is filled with blood.

Foreskin: the outer layer of skin along the shaft of the penis and over the tip, or head, of the penis.

Genes: the characteristics inherited from biological parents.

Genitals (Genitalia): a boy's external reproductive organs.

Growth spurt: a time of accelerated growth due to hormone changes during puberty.

Gynecomastia: sensitivity and potential swelling in the nipples caused by hormone changes during puberty.

Heredity: the passing of traits from parents to children.

Hormones: chemical messengers prompting change in the body, namely growth and maturity during puberty.

Insomnia: a clinical diagnosis for trouble falling asleep at night.

Melanin: the pigment giving us the color of our skin.

Mental health: well-being with regards to the mind, including emotions, intelligence, and life lessons.

Mood swings: emotional ups and downs common during puberty.

Nurture: to provide for a child's physical, mental, and social well-being.

Peer pressure: the influence from members of a similar age group.

Penis: the main organ of male genitalia.

Physical health: well-being with regards to the body, including food, exercise, sleep, shelter, and safety.

Pituitary gland: located in the brain; a main part of the endocrine system which prompts the release of growth hormones.

Puberty: the period of physical growth where the body sexually matures and becomes able to reproduce.

Razor burn: a painful irritation where body hair drops below the first layer of skin and creates bumps or ingrown hair.

Reproduction: the process where living organisms make offspring, or more of their kind.

Scoliosis: a common medical condition where a person's spine has a sideways curve.

Scrotum: the sack of skin that contains the testicles.

Self-exam: an examination of your own body, especially as a checkup for change.

Semen: the fluid that contains sperm cells.

Sex: when two people have close, intimate, naked contact.

Sexting: sending sexual pictures or texts to another person.

Sleep deprivation: sleep loss or insufficient sleep.

Social health: well-being with regards to interpersonal communication, including family, friends, and larger groups in society.

Sperm: the microscopic cells that contain a man's DNA.

Testicles (Testes): the two oval organs that produce sperm, enclosed in the scrotum behind the penis.

Testosterone: a hormone, produced mainly in the testes, responsible for male sex characteristics and growth.

Wet dreams (Nocturnal emissions): the release of semen, the fluid that contains sperm cells, in an overnight process.

RESOURCES

Chapter 1: These Changing Times

"All About Puberty." KidsHealth. Nemours Foundation.
October 2015. KidsHealth.org/en/kids/puberty.html

"Top Signs Boys Are In Puberty." Amaze. March 2019.
Amaze.org/video/top-signs-boys-are-in-puberty/

Chapter 2: Your Changing Body

"Body Mass Index (BMI)." KidsHealth. Nemours Foundation.
September 2015. KidsHealth.org/en/kids/bmi.html

"Why Do I Get Acne?" TeensHealth. Nemours Foundation.
June 2014. KidsHealth.org/en/teens/acne.html

Chapter 3: Looking and Sounding Older

"Gynecomastia." TeensHealth. Nemours Foundation. October
2016. KidsHealth.org/en/teens/boybrst.html

Natterson, Cara. *Guy Stuff: The Body Book for Boys.*
Middleton, WI: American Girl Publishing, 2017.

Chapter 4: Below the Belt

Advocates For Youth. Amaze. March 2019. Amaze.org/jr

Madaras, Lynda. *The "What's Happening to My Body" Book
For Boys.* New York, NY: New Market Press, 2007.

"Male Reproductive System." TeensHealth. Nemours Foundation. September 2016. KidsHealth.org/en/teens /male-repro.html

Sex, Etc. Answer. March 2019. SexEtc.org

Stay Teen. Power To Decide. March 2019. StayTeen.org

Chapter 5: Feeding and Fueling Your Body

Cronometer: Track Your Nutrition, Fitness, & Health Data. Cronometer. March 2019. Cronometer.com

"How Much Sleep Do We Really Need?" National Sleep Foundation. March 2019. SleepFoundation.org/excessive -sleepiness/support/how-much-sleep-do-we-really-need

"What is MyPlate?" ChooseMyPlate. March 2019. ChooseMyPlate.gov/WhatIsMyPlate

"Your Heart & Circulatory System." KidsHealth. Nemours Foundation. May 2018. KidsHealth.org/en/kids/heart.html

Chapter 6: Feelings and Friends

"Sexual Attraction and Orientation." TeensHealth. Nemours Foundation. October 2015. KidsHealth.org/en/teens /sexual-orientation.html

"What Consent Looks Like." RAINN. RAINN.org/articles /what-is-consent

"What Is Consent?" Love Is Respect. March 2019. LoveIsRespect.org/healthy-relationships/what-consent

Chapter 7: Family and Other Safe Spaces

Advocates For Youth. Amaze. March 2019. Amaze.org/jr

"Internet Safety Tips For Kids." Safe Search Kids. March 2019. SafeSearchKids.com/internet-safety-tips-for-kids

"Puberty." Young Men's Health. July 2017. YoungMensHealthSite.org/guides/puberty

Stay Teen. Power To Decide. March 2019. StayTeen.org

"Why Am I In Such a Bad Mood?" TeensHealth. Nemours Foundation. August 2015. KidsHealth.org/en/teens/bad-mood.html

REFERENCES

Chapter 1: These Changing Times

"All About Puberty." *KidsHealth*. Nemours Foundation. October 2015. https://kidshealth.org/en/kids/puberty.html

Bailey, Jacqui, and Jan McCafferty. *Sex, Puberty, and All that Stuff*. Hauppauge, NY: Barrons Educational Series, 2004.

"Boys and Puberty." *KidsHealth*. Nemours Foundation. September 2014. https://kidshealth.org/en/kids /boys-puberty.html

"The Changing Face of America's Adolescents." *U.S. Department of Health & Human Services*. February 2019. https://www.hhs.gov/ash/oah/facts-and-stats /changing-face-of-americas-adolescents/index.html

"Coming of Age: Adolescent Health." *World Health Organization*. February 2019. https://www.who.int/health -topics/adolescents/coming-of-age-adolescent-health

Madaras, Lynda. *The "What's Happening to My Body?" Book for Boys*. New York, NY: Newmarket Press, 2007.

McCave, Marta. *Puberty's Wild Ride*. Philadelphia, PA: Family Planning Council, 2004.

"Puberty." *Encyclopedia of Children's Health*. http://www.healthofchildren.com/P/Puberty.html

"Puberty." *Young Men's Health.* July 2017.
https://youngmenshealthsite.org/guides/puberty

"What is Puberty?" *WebMD.* WebMD, LLC. October 2017.
https://teens.webmd.com/boys/qa/what-is-puberty

Chapter 2: Your Changing Body

"Modern Human Diversity—Skin Color." *Smithsonian National
Museum of Natural History.* March 2019. http://humanorigins
.si.edu/evidence/genetics/human-skin-color-variation
/modern-human-diversity-skin-color

"Shortest Man Ever." *Guinness Book of World Records.*
March 2019. http://www.guinnessworldrecords.com
/world-records/67521-shortest-man-ever

"Skin Conditions By the Numbers." *American Academy of
Dermatology Association.* March 2019. https://www.aad.org
/media/stats/conditions/skin-conditions-by-the-numbers

"Tallest Man Ever." *Guinness Book of World Records.* March
2019. http://www.guinnessworldrecords.com/world-records
/tallest-man-ever

"Why Do I Get Acne?" *TeensHealth.* Nemours Foundation.
June 2014. https://kidshealth.org/en/teens/acne.html

Chapter 3: Looking and Sounding Older

Geggel, Laura. "Why Do Men Have Nipples?" *Live Science.*
June 2017. https://www.livescience.com/32467-why-do-men
-have-nipples.html

"Gynecomastia." *TeensHealth*. Nemours Foundation. October 2016. https://kidshealth.org/en/teens/boybrst.html

"What's an Adam's Apple?" *KidsHealth*. Nemours Foundation. June 2016. https://kidshealth.org/en/kids/adams-apple.html

"Why Is My Voice Changing?" *TeensHealth*. Nemours Foundation. June 2015. https://kidshealth.org/en/teens/voice-changing.html

Chapter 4: Below the Belt

"Male Reproductive System." *TeensHealth*. Nemours Foundation. September 2016. https://kidshealth.org/en/teens/male-repro.html

"Physical Development in Boys: What to Expect." *American Academy of Pediatrics*. May 2015. https://www.healthychildren.org/English/ages-stages/gradeschool/puberty/Pages/Physical-Development-Boys-What-to-Expect.aspx

"Testicular Exams." *TeensHealth*. Nemours Foundation. September 2016. https://kidshealth.org/en/teens/testicles.html

"What Are Wet Dreams?" *TeensHealth*. Nemours Foundation. September 2016. https://kidshealth.org/en/teens/expert-wet-dreams.html

Chapter 5: Feeding and Fueling Your Body

Butler, Natalie. "6 Essential Nutrients and Why Your Body Needs Them." *Healthline*. April 2018. https://www.healthline.com/health/food-nutrition/six-essential-nutrients

Comprehensive Implementation Plan on Maternal, Infant and Young Child Nutrition. Geneva: World Health Organization, 2014.

Global Action Plan For the Prevention and Control of NCDs 2013–2020. Geneva: World Health Organization, 2013.

Guideline: Sugars Intake for Adults and Children. Geneva: World Health Organization, 2015.

Hartwig, Melissa; Hartwig, Dallas. *The Whole30: The 30-Day Guide to Total Health and Food Freedom*. Boston, MA: Houghton Mifflin Harcourt, 2015.

"Healthy Diet." *World Health Organization*. October 2018. https://www.who.int/en/news-room/fact-sheets/detail/healthy-diet

Honeycutt, Emily. "Eating the Rainbow: Why Eating a Variety of Fruits and Vegetables Is Important for Optimal Health." *Food Revolution Network*. December 2017. https://foodrevolution.org/blog/eating-the-rainbow-health-benefits

"How Much Sleep Do We Really Need?" *National Sleep Foundation*. March 2019. https://www.sleepfoundation.org/excessive-sleepiness/support/how-much-sleep-do-we-really-need

"Nutrients." *World Health Organization.* March 2019.
https://www.who.int/elena/nutrient/en

Walker, Matthew. *Why We Sleep.* New York, NY: Simon &
Schuster, Inc., 2017.

"What is MyPlate?" *ChooseMyPlate.* March 2019.
https://www.choosemyplate.gov/WhatIsMyPlate

Chapter 6: Feelings and Friends

Ackerman, Courtney. "Essential Positive Coping
Skills." *Positive Psychology.* February 2019.
https://positivepsychologyprogram.com/coping-skills

Cherry, Kendra. "Color Psychology: Does It Affect How You
Feel?" *Very Well Mind.* March 2019. https://www.verywellmind
.com/color-psychology-2795824

Rough, Bonnie J. *Beyond Birds & Bees.* New York, NY: Seal
Press, 2018.

"Sexual Attraction and Orientation." *TeensHealth.* Nemours
Foundation. October 2015. https://kidshealth.org/en/teens
/sexual-orientation.html

Siegel, Dan. "The Healthy Mind Platter." *The Healthy Mind
Platter.* 2011. https://www.drdansiegel.com/resources
/healthy_mind_platter/

"What Consent Looks Like." *RAINN.* https://www.rainn.org
/articles/what-is-consent

"What Is Consent?" *Love Is Respect.* March 2019. https://www
.loveisrespect.org/healthy-relationships/what-consent/

Chapter 7: Family and Other Safe Spaces

"Adolescent Mental Health." *World Health Organization.* September 2018. https://www.who.int/news-room /fact-sheets/detail/adolescent-mental-health

"Child and Adolescent Mental Health." *National Institutes of Health.* April 2017. https://www.nimh.nih.gov/health/topics /child-and-adolescent-mental-health/index.shtml

"Why Am I in Such a Bad Mood?" *TeensHealth.* Nemours Foundation. August 2015. https://kidshealth.org/en/teens /bad-mood.html

INDEX

ACKNOWLEDGMENTS

I didn't expect to brave another journey through adolescence in this lifetime, but puberty managed to find me once again. This time I was a little more prepared with both a sense of humor and a sense of respect. Growing up is often something we try to rush through . . . until, of course, we're all grown up and we wish we had a do-over. This is my do-over. I hope it helps young people and their families open up important conversations about the greatest subject in the world: life.

This couldn't have happened without fellow educators helping push for comprehensive health programs and accessible, appropriate resources for kids and teens. Many thanks to the men who contributed quotes for these chapters, and to all of the referenced organizations for their leadership in health education.

Thank you to my wife, Sarah, for the unending support; to my family for showing me the way into education; to my children for letting me see the world with a new lens; and to my students for teaching me how to stay young. Final thanks go out to you, the reader, for putting your trust in these words as you become that person who will pass on his knowledge and experience to the future. No matter what age, may we all continue the journey of *growing up great*.

ABOUT THE AUTHOR

Scott Todnem has been teaching Health Education at the middle school level since 2001. He was named the 2019 National Health Teacher of the Year. He is a nationally recognized presenter who travels to speak about the benefits of great health education programs. He has led educational trips to the state and nation's capitals, worked as team-building coordinator for students and staff, and served as a summer camp coordinator for young people. He has also served as part of inclusive committees for cultural and gender diversity and uses his platforms for mental health awareness and suicide prevention.

Scott grew up in a few locations stateside and overseas, meeting new friends from various walks of life. He developed an eclectic list of interests and hobbies, falling in love with everything from sports to comic books, from poetry to punk rock. Scott was always a bit tall, a bit sensitive, and just a little bit awkward.

He currently resides in Illinois with his wife and four children, where he enjoys reading, record collecting, and making the best/worst Dad jokes possible.

Additional writing and other content can be found on his website, LifeIsTheFuture.com. You can find him on social media as @MrTodnem or @ScottAmpersand.

CPSIA information can be obtained
at www.ICGtesting.com
Printed in the USA
JSHW021823140220
4239JS00002B/2